Drive and...

Lincolnshire

·

Roger Fox

COUNTRYSIDE BOOKS
NEWBURY BERKSHIRE

First published 2006
© Roger Fox, 2006

COUNTRYSIDE BOOKS
3 Catherine Road
Newbury, Berkshire

To view our complete range of books,
please visit us at
www.countrysidebooks.co.uk

ISBN 1 85306 955 8
EAN 978 1 85306 955 0

Cover picture of the Ramblers' church,
Walesby, supplied by Bill Meadows

Photographs by the author

Designed by Peter Davies, Nautilus Design
Produced through MRM Associates Ltd., Reading
Printed by Borcombe Printers plc, Romsey

Contents

AREA MAP SHOWING LOCATIONS OF THE WALKS

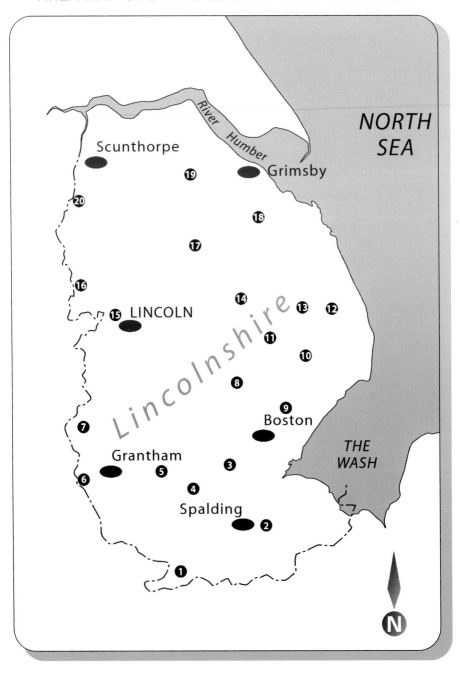

Contents ✍

Publisher's Note

We hope that you obtain considerable enjoyment from this book; great care has been taken in its preparation. Although at the time of publication all routes followed public rights of way or permitted paths, diversion orders can be made and permissions withdrawn.

We cannot, of course, be held responsible for such diversion orders and any inaccuracies in the text which result from these or any other changes to the routes nor any damage which might result from walkers trespassing on private property. We are anxious though that all details covering the walks are kept up to date and would therefore welcome information from readers which would be relevant to future editions.

The simple sketch maps that accompany the walks in this book are based on notes made by the author whilst checking out the routes on the ground. However, for the benefit of a proper map, we do recommend that you purchase the relevant Ordnance Survey sheet covering your walk. The Ordnance Survey maps are widely available, especially through booksellers and local newsagents.

Introduction

Lincolnshire is a land full of secrets and surprises, a little bit of everything and something for everyone. Those who dismiss this county as a flat and uninteresting region of reclaimed fens should venture into the hilly wolds that so inspired the poetry of Alfred Lord Tennyson. Those who believe this to be a cultural backwater are reminded that the cathedral crowning Lincoln's limestone ridge is arguably England's finest Gothic masterpiece – a sight of more splendour does not exist throughout the realm.

It is not only the Poet Laureate whose thoughts have been provoked by these surroundings. It was at Woolsthorpe near Grantham that the truths of gravity and motion descended upon Sir Isaac Newton; and in Grantham itself lived Margaret Roberts, who was to become Lady Thatcher. John Wesley, the founder of Methodism, grew up in the Isle of Axholme, and countless Lincolnshire pioneers include the Pilgrim Fathers and Captain John Smith, the Willoughby explorer famous for his adventures with Pocohontas.

Lincolnshire will reveal to you castles at Old Bolingbroke and Lincoln; mystical monastic ruins at Crowland and Thornton Abbey; restored windmill towers whose number runs into double figures; and picturesque watermill settings like Cogglesford and Stockwith.

But it is for the medieval churches found in every town and village that Lincolnshire has become renowned. The ornate pinnacles and spires of Kesteven, the colossal 'galleons' of Holland's fenland and the patchwork shrines of Lindsey and the Wolds cover every architectural period with a completeness not found in any other county. Boston's 'Stump' is the country's loftiest parish church tower and Louth church has the tallest spire.

The towns and villages in which these historic gems are found are linked by an intricate network of footpaths and tracks crossing Lincolnshire's unspoilt landscape of rolling farmland and ancient woodland. These twenty walks embrace the whole range of rural settings, from canal towpaths to forgotten green lanes and disused railtracks. Most of the walks contain sections where it would be advisable to wear boots, and a few paths are beset by encroaching undergrowth which shows no respect for ramblers or their rights of way.

All of the walks either start near a good pub or tea room where you can enjoy a meal after your outing or there is a refreshment stop just a short drive away. Other places providing food and drink are mentioned, and telephone numbers are also shown so you can check availability.

Now, the little-trodden byways and rich fertile countryside of Lincolnshire are calling. There is a magic around these hidden villages and windswept heights, and the colours of snowdrops, bluebells, daffodils and hawthorn berries beckon. The friendliest of welcomes is guaranteed from the folk of Lincolnshire, to whose enthusiasm and encouragement I owe so much while I have compiled these chapters. Finally a special debt of gratitude must be expressed to Nigel, who taught me that there is so much more to life. Enjoy your stroll!

Roger Fox

1 | Greatford and Braceborough

Braceborough

The Walk 3½ miles
Terrain Level walking throughout.
Map OS Explorer 234 Rutland Water or Landranger 130 Grantham
(GR 086118)

How to get there

Greatford is situated 4 miles north-east of Stamford and is clearly signed from three major roads – the A16 at Tallington, the A15 at Baston and the A6121 at Carlby. **Parking:** At the Hare and Hounds pub in Greatford, with permission or park considerately by the roadside.

Drive and Stroll

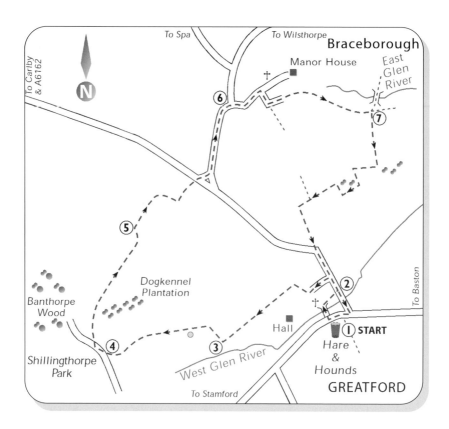

Introduction

The villages around Stamford, where the fens rise gently to rolling hills, are brimming with cottages, halls and inns built of local mellow limestone rivalling anything the Cotswolds have to offer. Greatford is one such village, sited at the confluence of the east and west branches of the River Glen and a popular halt along the Macmillan Way long-distance path – one garden here even boasts a thatched summer-house. A handsome inn with a reputation for first-class food is the ideal base for an exploration of the rural paths linking Greatford with its neighbour, Braceborough. Both villages have tales to tell, while Greatford Hall introduces you to a sculptor with a sense of humour and a doctor of famous royal patronage.

The Hare and Hounds

This stone-built pub lives up to the standards imposed by the rest of the village. Though it is mainly laid out for dining, locals gather around the bar where a broad selection of real ales is on offer. The menus rotate seasonally and might include venison in orange and port or roast guinea fowl, with home-made fruit crumble to follow. A choice of roasts replaces the menus on Sundays, and the meals are excellent enough to make booking advisable. One word of warning: to retain its traditional ambience and make the most of its position on the Macmillan Way, a good-natured fine is levied for every mobile phone heard ringing, with all proceeds donated to the Macmillan nurses. Normal opening times apply except for Sunday evenings and Mondays, when the pub remains closed. Food is served between the hours of 12 noon and 2 pm and again from 6 pm to 9 pm. Telephone: 01778 560332.

THE WALK

Pay close attention, please, because on leaving the Hare and Hounds you are immediately surrounded by this outing's quirkiest features – and tremendous fun is to be had spotting them. The centre of Greatford is adorned by the stone carvings of Major Fitzwilliam, owner of the hall in the 1930s. Two giant coronets in the gardens opposite start you off. No more clues – I will leave you to discover the mushrooms, obelisks, fonts and friezes around you. Turn left, walk over the road and cross the bridge leading you towards the church. The **West Glen River** here appears as a canal running past the opulent outbuildings of **Greatford Hall** into the grounds behind.

Greatford Hall became the private asylum of Doctor Francis Willis for 'afflicted persons of distinction and respectability'. Willis famously cured 'the madness of King George' in 1788 and the church contains a marble monument by Nollekens in his memory. Willis's sons attended further outbreaks of the king's insanity, but with less success. Shillingthorpe Hall was also used by the doctor as a mental hospital. After a fire in 1931, the Hall was rebuilt by Major Fitzwilliam, the creator of the village's unusual sculptures.

The church itself maintains the village's high standard of stonework – the splendid broach spire is unusually positioned above the south transept. Cross the churchyard to locate a narrow passageway leading from its corner. Along here a shaded stream is crossed before a kissing gate returns you to the road.

Now turn left, then left again into a new avenue named **Greatford Gardens**, accompanied by the sound of the

Drive and Stroll

The Hare and Hounds in Greatford.

splashing stream. Proceed as far as the Hall gates, where a narrow hedged footpath on your right leads you between the grounds of the Hall and a private garden. Cross a footbridge and enter a long narrow belt of woodland, which you follow to the left for a third of a mile.

③

Emerging from the trees the path continues to the right along the edge of arable farmland until a footpath sign ushers you into another field on your left. The path across here is clear and slants half-right through the crop, passing a small pond on the left. Through the clear gap in the hedgerow ahead, the path adjusts to cross the next field on a more direct bearing, aiming for a huge oak

beneath which a stile takes you into a meadow. Diagonally to the right across this meadow seek another stile leading you once more into wooded surroundings. Join the track running through this wood and follow it to the right until you find yourself at the edge of a grassy tract.

You may remark that the trees and meadows around you have a more cultivated appearance than the adjacent countryside. This is because you are standing in Shillingthorpe Park – the grounds of the long vanished Hall of the same name. A few evocative stone walls, remains of brick buildings and a moat may be spotted, but today the pheasants are the only inmates of Doctor Willis' former sanatorium.

(4)

A clear footpath sign diverts you half-right, where a good track across the meadow targets the gap between **Banthorpe Wood** and **Dogkennel Plantation**. Cross the following meadow in the same direction and continue along a clear path across the next arable field. Over a railed footbridge follow the edge of the next field to its left.

(5)

Turn right at the field's corner and now join a row of tall trees along the winding border of this field to arrive eventually at another road. Cross the road, proceed along the lane branching off it signed for **Braceborough** and stroll into this sleepy stone village.

Braceborough enjoyed fleeting fame as a spa resort during the 19th century, pumping 1,500,000 gallons of its healing waters daily through the spa foundation. The spa soon faded from favour, however, and closed in 1938.

(6)

At a junction by the Victorian school, a sign points towards the church and you should follow the indicated lane past a number of grand houses as far as the church, whose surrounding yew trees are illuminated in autumn by bright red berries. After looking around, retrace your steps along the lane but turn left onto a lesser lane – the only branch along here. Follow this lane as it bends left by a thatched cottage but at the next bend continue straight ahead through the farmyard and onto the track beyond. Remain on this exhilarating open track until the **East Glen River** comes close by on your left.

(7)

At this point the right of way heads straight across the field on your right, rejoining the route of the **Macmillan Way** and aiming for the right-hand edge of the wood ahead. Reaching the hedgerow cross the footbridge, turn right and begin to pursue the good path around the edge of this field. A short distance beyond another small wood, the path angles left – still tracing the boundary of the same field – and soon joins a road coming in from the right. It is now less than ⅓ mile along this road to your starting point in the centre of **Greatford**.

Place of Interest Nearby

Grimsthorpe Castle, 10 miles to the north, dates from medieval times and displays fine examples of the work of Sir John Vanbrugh and Capability Brown. Telephone: 01778 591205.

2 Moulton and Whaplode

The Moulton windmill houses an excellent tearoom

The Walk 3½ miles
Terrain Good surfaces, with one short grassy path and not a hill in sight.
Map OS Explorer 249 Spalding and Holbeach or Landranger 131 Boston and Spalding (GR 307241).

How to get there

Moulton is easy to find midway between Spalding and Holbeach on the A151. The walk begins at the windmill in the heart of the village by the green ½ mile to the south. **Parking:** There is plenty of room along the roads around Moulton's village green.

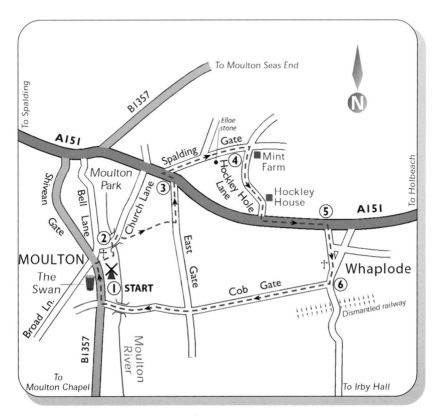

Introduction

In the vast open landscape of the Lincolnshire fens, Moulton is an oasis of greenery. The village's windmill, visible for miles around, forms the focus of this gentle stroll around the lanes. Restored to its former splendour, the windmill boasts the country's loftiest tower and houses an excellent little tearoom on the bare wooden boards of one of its levels. Historic churches in Moulton and the neighbouring village of Whaplode are taken in, along with a curious carved Anglo-Saxon tablet. You will enjoy seeking out the modern sculptures dotted around Whaplode, and orchids will be among the plants you see growing in the fields by the quiet back lanes.

Drive and Stroll

The Granary Tearoom

The restoration of the windmill in 2005 included the introduction of the Granary Tearoom on the windmill's first floor. Cream teas and delicious cakes can be enjoyed here and, by the summer of 2006, the menu will have been extended to include soups, sandwiches and a selection of hot meals. Jams, souvenirs and paintings are on sale, soon to be joined by flours ground on the premises under the power of wind. The tearoom is open between 10 am and 4 pm from Thursday to Sunday, and on Bank Holidays. Telephone: 01406 373237.

If the windmill is not open, the Swan in Moulton also serves fine meals.

THE WALK

Start the walk by heading for the churchyard. From its corner, a signed footpath slants across the grounds of the church – more an arboretum than a graveyard. Reaching the **Moulton River** turn left onto **Church Walk** to pass a pair of old cottages, then right when you reach **Church Lane**.

Now pass three houses on your right before veering into an opening towards the wide fields of the fens and taking up the footpath alongside the hedge, now on your left. This grassy path is the sole section of the walk not on a metalled surface, and you soon reach another lane named **Eastgate** – turn left here.

At the busy A151 cross with care and stroll left for a few paces before turning right into **Spalding Gate** and re-entering rural surroundings. Having passed Wood Lane on the left you come to a neat little hedge on the right. Within this hedge stands the ancient **Elloe Stone**, badly weathered and mounted on a plinth.

The Elloe Stone marks the spot where the court of the Wapentake assembled in the 10th and 11th centuries.

Continue to the crossroads at **Mint Farm** and turn right into **Hockley Hole Lane**. Just past **Hockley House** turn left at the A151. The next village, **Whaplode**, announces itself as 'A Village with Sculptures' and the large wrought-iron flower painted bright yellow is the first of these.

Turn right into **Kirkgate** towards the village centre. Opposite the carved pig named the 'Whapplehog', on the right, is **St Mary's**, another church of great splendour and warranting a lengthy examination. Leave the churchyard, continue past the vicarage and turn right into **Cob Gate** – though you may first wish to walk as far as the dismantled railway trackbed to view more sculptures. Even further in this direction is **Irby Hall**, the former home of Sir Anthony Irby, whose impressive memorial graces the church.

Even in an area famous for fine churches, St Mary's in Whaplode stands out. It is a treasure trove of architecture from all periods and reflects the village's prosperity when the fens here were first reclaimed in the 13th century. Of particular interest is the Irby Memorial, commemorating Sir Anthony and Elizabeth Irby. Recently repainted, the effigies of the couple are surrounded by their six children, shown kneeling in line. The tower, like those at nearby Long Sutton and Fleet, is detached from the main body of the church.

Now stride out of **Whaplode** along **Cob Gate**, from which ever-improving views of Moulton's windmill and spire can be enjoyed. Remain on Cob Gate for a full mile, crossing **East Gate** midway and turning right into **High Street** when you re-enter **Moulton**. Now back to the windmill – time for an ascent of the tower and your reward in the tearoom!

Built in 1822, Moulton's windmill is the tallest in the land. A team of local enthusiasts have worked hard, and now the tower, complete with dazzling white cap, has been restored to its height of over 100 feet.

Places of Interest Nearby

In Spalding, **Ayscoughee Hall** is a 15th-century wool merchant's house converted into a series of outstanding galleries, one of which is devoted to the story of the drainage of the fens. It is set in beautiful gardens famous for their yew walls. Telephone: 01775 712657.

More fen drainage history can be discovered at the **Pinchbeck Engine & Drainage Museum**, where you can see a restored working beam engine of 1833. Telephone: 01775 725468.

South of Whaplode is the **Museum of Entertainment**, whose collection includes fairground and barrel organs, Victorian music boxes and Edison phonographs. Telephone: 01406 540379.

Drive and Stroll

The Red Lion

Built in 1665 the Red Lion has been serving travellers on the road from Boston to Grantham for centuries. Today, the meals are of high quality, generous and all home-cooked. Scarlet lions guard the entrance door but the atmosphere inside is friendly and welcoming. A menu of the usual expected dishes is supplemented by 'specials' chalked onto a wallboard, and a good selection of real ales is available, including Adnam's Broadside and Directors. The Sunday lunch carvery is very popular and booking is recommended. Meals are served from 12 noon to 2.30 pm and from 6.30 pm to 9.30 pm. Telephone: 01775 821950.

THE WALK

From the Red Lion strike out along **Red Lion Street**, pass **Vine House** and halt at a small grassy island, where an old tree shelters a circle of wooden seating. Turn right into **School Lane** and follow this to the next junction by the Methodist chapel, built in 1908, and featuring a bold stained-glass window. Here you will also spot the restored village pump and a memorial to the men of the village lost in both World Wars.

You are now following the **Old Eau**, the watercourse wending its way through the heart of the village. Proceed along the lane on the stream's left (**High Street**), passing in turn a converted Wesleyan chapel, a well-kept terrace of Victorian houses and the former White Horse Inn. Where High Street becomes **Gauntlet Road**, continue straight ahead past a row of whitewashed cottages, one of which is the post office. Beyond the **White Swan** the lane becomes more open and the buildings and trees more sparse.

Half a mile along here the lane terminates and the option to return along the Old Eau's opposite bank may be selected. But a short extension into the rural heartland of the fens – still pursuing the course of the Old Eau – is recommended. Turn left into **Back Lane** and stroll for almost 1 mile until you reach **Bicker Gauntlet**, passing the first of two farms named **Gauntlet Farm**. Here are extensive views towards the church spires of Donington and Swineshead.

Cross the stream at the first opportunity to commence the return journey along **Fore Lane**. Eventually this lane crooks right to cross **Back Lane** and heads back towards the village, now on **Cemetery Road** on the Old Eau's eastern bank. Just past the black and gold railings of the cemetery itself, the crisp Georgian **Bicker Manor**, dating from the 1770s, may be admired. The Old Vicarage is the next house, followed naturally by St Swithin's church, whose treasures may delay you for some time.

The Red Lion at Bicker was built in 1665.

 ⑤

Soon enough you arrive back at the War Memorial, from which you retrace your earlier steps to **Red Lion Street**. Do not, however, complete the outing on your original route but divert left into **Morley Lane**, the narrowest of roads, with the stream still alongside and a pleasing end to your day's walking. Along here several more fine buildings will arrest your attention, including a splendid ivy-clad grange complete with clipped yews and ha-ha, before you find yourself once more outside the **Red Lion**.

The navigable estuary of Bicker Haven, an arm of the Wash, reached as far as the Red Lion once upon a time – this explains the village's former prosperity and the impressive church. Three miles south-east of here the Haven was marked by huge mounds created by medieval salt making, forming higher ground in this flat landscape.

Places of Interest Nearby

There is much to see and do in **Boston**, including a visit to the 'Slump' – at 272 feet this claims to be England's tallest church tower. The **Maud Foster Windmill** has been restored to full working order while the **Guildhall Museum** chronicles the fascinating history of the town. Another working windmill can be found at **Heckington**, 8 miles away; and nearby **Donington** is the birthplace of 18th-century navigator Matthew Flinders. Telephone Boston Tourist Information Office for details: 01205 356656.

4 Pointon and Sempringham Priory

St Andrew's church in Sempringham is an unexpected find.

The Walk 3 miles
Terrain Good rural tracks and surfaced lanes, with some gentle gradients.
Map OS Explorer 248 Bourne and Heckington or Landranger 130 Grantham (GR 117320)

How to get there

Heading north from Bourne on the A15, the B1177 to Heckington branches off to the right after 3 miles and Pointon is found just 4 miles along here. **Parking:** At the Old Ship inn, with permission.

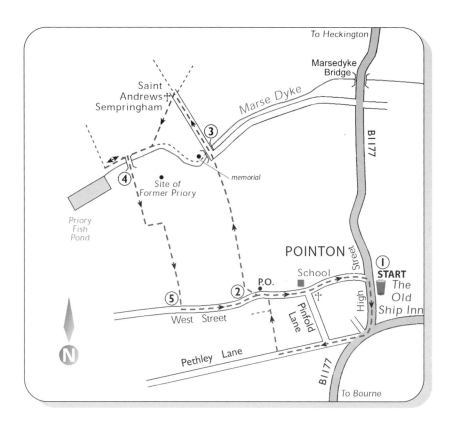

Introduction

Away from the winding road linking the fen villages between Heckington and Bourne is the loneliest of lanes. Amid the solitude and desolation, at the end of this track, stands a huge medieval church, near to the spot where Lincolnshire's most important monastery once thrived – Sempringham Priory. The priory has vanished almost entirely, but an ccric atmosphere lingers, and a walk through these holy acres is the perfect way to experience this moody silence.

Drive and Stroll

The Old Ship

This fine stone inn by the roadside in Pointon is stylishly decorated in a contemporary style. In addition to the lounge, you will find an airy conservatory, a further dining area and lots of room on the lawns outside. Real ales are served here – for example, Elgood's Golden Newt and Abbot Ale – as well as a wide selection of fine wines. The menus offer some out of the ordinary ideas – the local venison and steak in a wild berry sauce are popular. The meals are all of a very high quality and delightfully presented, and are available from 12 noon to 2.30 pm (closed Monday lunchtime) and from 6 pm to 9 pm. Telephone: 01529 241400.

THE WALK

From the Old Ship Inn walk left along Pointon's **High Street** until the road sweeps right. Here turn into **Pethley Lane** on the right to find yourself immediately in open countryside. Pass **Pinfold Lane** on the right and after 200 yards, a signed footpath cuts between two arable fields before a cobbled driveway between new houses takes you onto **West Street**.

Follow **West Street** to the left as far as a tiny post office on the right at which a kissing gate directs you onto a short diagonal path through the scrub to another kissing gate. A grassy footpath between fields of crops now stretches ahead of you for ½ mile, truly exposed and rising gently. Along here the tower of **St Andrew's** looms dramatically into view. Continue down the hill, over a footbridge and along a hedgerow to a lonely lane. Cross the **Marse Dyke** and halt at an unexpected memorial on the left.

The lane now leads you to the gates of **St Andrew's**, a church of beauty and romance and a most unexpected find.

At a stile a shortcut leads from the corner of the churchyard across a field to the lonely lane by the **Marse Dyke**, but if this path is overgrown simply return to the memorial and turn right. It is worth following the lane as far as a sharp right-hand bend. Here, amongst the undergrowth to the left, is what was once the abbey fishponds.

④

Now turn back along the lane, cross the **Marse Dyke** by the wide bridge and pursue the farm track up the hillside. The grassy mounds in the field on your left mark the site of the long vanished priory. The track heads to the left near the field's highest point. From here the best views over the whole of the medieval layout are spread before you. The track then continues back to **West Street** in Pointon.

Turn left and follow **West Street** back to **High Street**. Beyond the post office look out for the Victorian school crowned by a stone bell turret, the restored village pump and a tiny church of black corrugated iron, neatly trimmed in white and also boasting a bell turret. Not far from here **High Street** is reached, with the **Old Ship Inn** directly opposite you.

The memorial to Gwenllian, Sempringham.

Places of Interest Nearby

The magnificent eight-sailed windmill at **Heckington** is open to the public and a range of flours produced here can be purchased. Telephone: 01529 461919.

The neighbouring village of **Folkingham** still retains the earthworks of its Norman castle, a 19th-century House of Correction and the village stocks and whipping post – as well as a shop selling irresistible home-made chocolates!

5 | Newton and Haceby

The award-winning Red Lion in Newton.

The Walk 4½ miles
Terrain Roads, field paths and a few gentle hills.
Map OS Explorer 248 Bourne and Heckington or Landranger 130 Grantham (GR 045361)

How to get there

Locate the roundabout 6 miles south of Sleaford where the A15 and the A52 cross. Drive west on the A52 towards Grantham and 1½ miles along here a signed lane leads off to the left into Newton. Turn right at the T-junction in the village and the Red Lion is on the right not far from here. **Parking:** Parking is limited in Newton. Ask for permission at the inn or park considerately on the street running above the south side of the village.

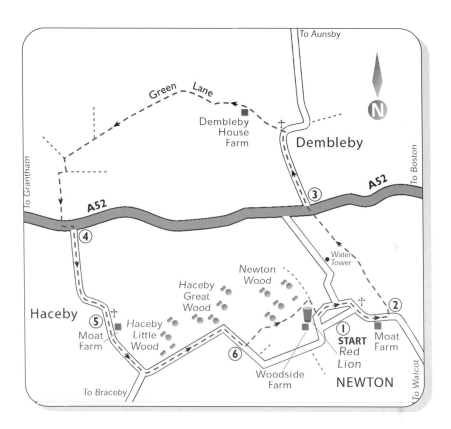

Introduction

Hidden away on the narrow lanes of Lincolnshire's stone belt can be found countless villages and hamlets of brick-red roof tiles and walls of mellow local stone. One of these villages is Newton, where a charming country inn thrives and an imposing church overlooks an old cross on the green below. Haceby, though, like Newton set in a secluded leafy hollow, is a mere hamlet, almost deserted. Serene lanes and tracks link these picturesque villages, passing ancient woodlands where deer may be spotted and if your timing is good, the most enormous conkers may be gathered!

Drive and Stroll

The Red Lion

This award-winning pub is a special place, a low, old stone building screened by willows and secluded to the point of being almost invisible. Yet, always popular and busy, the inn's reputation has clearly spread far and wide – booking is certainly advisable during busy periods. The menu revolves around the renowned cold carvery, though bar meals, lighter snacks and daily specials are also available. A hot carvery is added on Sundays and the real ales include Bateman's XB and a guest beer such as Woodforde's Wherry. As well as a warren of intimate dining areas the inn even boasts its own squash courts! The Red Lion is open during normal hours and meals are served from 12 noon to 2 pm and from 7 pm to 9 pm (6.30 pm to 9 pm on Saturdays). Telephone: 01529 497256.

THE WALK

①

The houses of **Newton** congregate around a central ellipse of lanes – **St Botolph's church** is at the point directly opposite the **Red Lion**, in a setting by the old stone cross. Locate the church and ascend the lane running alongside it, passing **Moat Farm** on the right and looking out for a public footpath sign on the left.

②

The path crossing the cow field from here leads you to another stile and footbridge, from which the path keeps a hedge on its left along the edges of the next two fields. When the hedge deserts you, the route angles slightly left across the following field to another footbridge to resume its way alongside the hedge. As you descend steeply to the A52, rabbits may scurry into the hedgerow or a hare race across the fields.

③

At the main road cross cautiously and proceed along the lane ahead, soon to reach the well-kept farming hamlet of **Dembleby**. Branch left at the church onto a quiet lane and follow this to **Dembleby House Farm**. The lane (known as **Green Lane**) now continues as a good farm track cutting through these gentle hills for an enjoyable mile. Continue straight ahead at a sign reading 'road used as a public path', now on a greener track and, at the meeting of ways beyond here, turn left then right, observing two more public path notices. Follow the track you are now on for only a few yards, turning left along the first hedgerow as indicated by a red waymarker. This footpath leads you back down to the A52.

④

To your left you will see a quiet lane on the opposite side of the road leading up the hillside – again, please cross carefully. Half a mile along here the road zigzags left and right to enter another tiny village hidden amongst the trees in the valley – the almost depopulated hamlet of **Haceby**. Like Newton, all is cream-coloured stone, including Haceby's brightest gem, the ancient **church of St Margaret**.

 ⑤

Continue past **Moat Farm** out of Haceby and turn left at a junction (signed Newton). Initially lined by horse chestnut trees (yielding excellent conker harvests) this broad-verged lane now guides you for about 1 mile. Along here you will count three distinct woods on your left, **Haceby Little Wood**, **Haceby Great Wood** and **Newton Wood**.

 ⑥

Beyond a sharp right-hand bend you will spot the first of two clear public footpath signs on your left. Cross the field, targeting the kissing gate at the corner of **Newton Wood**. The path now traces the edge of a meadow below the wood, followed by two smaller meadows adjacent to **Woodside Farm**. In the next meadow, now clear of the wood, turn to the right and stroll down to the stile – beneath, incidentally, the most prodigious conker tree of all! You now find yourself back in the village of **Newton**, close to the **Red Lion**.

Places of Interest Nearby

Sleaford is a small market town with a splendid church and the remains of a Norman castle, both dating from the 12th century. The **Hub**, on the site of the Sleaford Canal Navigation Wharf, houses a number of art and design galleries and the Riverside Café. Telephone: 01529 308710.

Cogglesford Mill, ½ mile to the east, is a working watermill producing flour which can be bought from the mill shop. Telephone: 01529 414294.

27

6 Woolsthorpe by Belvoir and the Grantham Canal

Strolling beside the Grantham Canal near Woolsthorpe.

The Walk 4½ miles
Terrain A variety of surfaces, with a few steep hillsides.
Map OS Explorer 247 Grantham or Landranger 130 Grantham
(GR 838341)

How to get there
Woolsthorpe by Belvoir is situated 4 miles west of Grantham, 2 miles from both the A52 and the A607. From the A607 turn off at Denton and follow the signs; from Muston on the A52 simply head south until you reach the village. **Parking:** On the roadside in Woolsthorpe's Main Street.

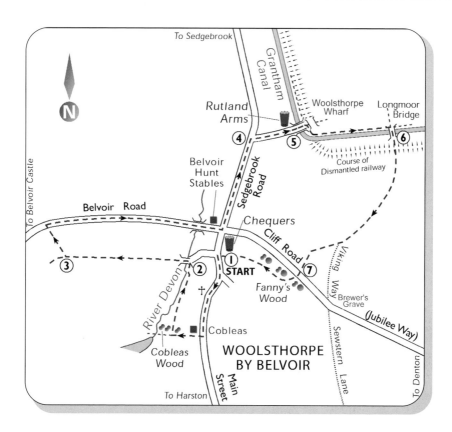

Introduction

In the shadow of Belvoir Castle lies the ducal village of Woolsthorpe, and behind the road rising up the hill through here can be found the Chequers, an award-winning inn providing the perfect base for a hearty walk. Sensational views of the castle, a tranquil canal towpath and sections of the Viking and Jubilee Ways – these are all included on your route, which passes through some of the most stunning scenery that Lincolnshire has to offer.

The Chequers

Overlooking the village cricket pitch, views to Belvoir Castle, and elegant surroundings matched only by the quality of the food – it's no wonder that the Chequers has won accolades from every major guide. Inside there are numerous dining areas to choose from, including the naked brick chamber

29

Drive and Stroll

of the former bakehouse. The menu limits itself to just a few options but they all sound so mouth-watering that choosing is still a dilemma – even the sausage and mash comes with a red wine sauce. Sandwiches are also served and traditional roasts replace the usual menus on Sundays. A good selection of real ales – including several locally brewed beers – are available and, after your meal, you can relax in the private garden or even try your hand at petanque. The Chequers is open from 12 noon to 3 pm and from 5.30 pm to 11 pm (12 noon to 7 pm on Sundays), and meals can be ordered from 12 noon to 2.30 pm and from 7 pm to 9.30 pm (12 noon to 4 pm on Sundays). Telephone: 01476 870701.

THE WALK

From the tiny Millennium Green, begin by climbing Woolsthorpe's **Main Street**, passing the stone school building and the lofty church tower. Only built in 1847, this church replaces the original St James', burnt down by the Roundheads during the Civil War. Reaching **Cobleas**, a row of bungalows on your right, turn into the lane signed 'Fishing Lakes'. Strolling down here, the first of the day's views of Belvoir Castle and the lakes themselves can be enjoyed. Spotting a public footpath sign, dive into the narrow wood on your right, soon to emerge at a stile on the edge of a pasture. The footpath makes its way towards the **River Devon** and hugs the waterside hedgerow through three such pastures, each exited via further stiles.

Reaching the single brick arch of a bridge the lane could be followed back into Woolsthorpe, but the extension over the stile on the other side of the bridge is thoroughly

recommended and should not be viewed as optional. Following the **Jubilee Way** the path climbs the grassy field to join the line of a hedge. From the hillside horizon **Belvoir Castle** rears up ahead of you like a scene from a medieval fairy tale – there must be a dozen turrets and towers serrating the skyline!

Commanding a spectacular view across the Vale of Belvoir, pronounced 'Beever', the castle has been destroyed and rebuilt many times since William the Conqueror gave this site to his standard bearer, Robert de Todeni. The seat of the Dukes of Rutland since the reign of Henry VIII, the castle houses art treasures by Rubens, Holbein and Reynolds, as well as an historic array of weaponry.

Arriving at a stile, the route continues on a narrow path between the fence and ditch on your right. However, to gain the most intimate views of the castle, it is first worth pursuing the track ahead until a notice forbids further progress. Back on the

The Chequers Inn, Woolsthorpe by Belvoir.

foothpath, turn right when you reach the road and march down the hill for almost 1 mile, admiring views in all directions and finally arriving at a crossroads. Turn left into **Sedgebrook Road** here, noting that the impressive range of buildings on the corner forms the stables of the Belvoir Hunt – the row of cottages opposite is named **Hunt Cottages**.

 ④

When you come to a sign for the **Rutland Arms** turn right and continue to the pub – also known locally as the Dirty Duck. This point on the Grantham Canal is **Woolsthorpe Wharf** and there is much activity here, though walkers, campers and cyclists have replaced the barges and locomotives that once passed by.

When the Grantham Canal was opened in 1797 the cost of transporting goods to and from Nottingham was drastically reduced. Barges carried grain and agricultural produce from Grantham, returning from Nottingham loaded with coal and building materials. Each village along the canal contributed to the trade by constructing its own wharf. In common with other canals, the arrival of the railways led to decline and in 1936 the canal was abandoned. Today the towpath has been revived as a cycle track and a campaign is in progress to restore and reopen the canal.

 ⑤

Cross the canal bridge by the lock-keeper's cottage and turn right

Drive and Stroll

through the kissing gate to join the towpath, passing two intact sets of lock gates. The scenery of open fields rising to wooded hillsides seen through the trees and bushes alongside the canal is enchanting, and all too soon you reach the ivy-clad brick arch of **Longmoor Bridge**.

Cross the bridge and climb the track through the trees on the opposite bank – note the sturdy piers of the former railway bridge on your right. The broad track, this time on the route of the **Viking Way**, climbs through an overhead tunnel of oak branches as it traces a large arc above the steep wooded valley of **Mickledales**. At the summit seek a public footpath sign on your right and enter the cornfield here – to continue along the track would take you to Brewer's Grave at the point where the Viking Way, the Jubilee Way and the ancient Sewstern Lane all meet. The field path first aims diagonally for the corner of a hedge, then straightens to target a gap in the hedge at the road below.

Cross the road and join the track leading into **Fanny's Wood** directly opposite. Reaching a clearing, cross the stile on your left and turn to the right, once more on grassy terrain. As you follow the edge of the wood on your right, final views may be savoured of the castle, now seen immediately above Woolsthorpe's church tower. Beyond the wood continue steeply downhill in the same direction and cross the stile behind the scoreboard to emerge next to the boundary of the cricket pitch overlooked by the Chequers. Now, will you stay and watch a few overs? Or take in a game of petanque, maybe? Perhaps you'll simply retire to the comfort of the inn, and place your order – you have deserved your reward.

Places of Interest Nearby

What better way to extend your outing than a visit to **Belvoir Castle** itself? As well as tours of the stately rooms there are extensive grounds and regular events. Telephone: 01476 871002.

    Grantham's museum is also a fascinating place to visit – displays about local luminaries Sir Isaac Newton and Lady Thatcher are featured here. Telephone: 01476 568783.

7 | Dry Doddington and Stubton

The Wheatsheaf Inn at Dry Doddington overlooks the village green.

The Walk 5 miles
Terrain Some gentle hills and field paths.
Map OS Explorer 271 Newark on Trent or Landranger 130 Grantham
(GR 850466)

How to get there

Dry Doddington is easily located 1 mile east of the A1 and 6 miles south of
Newark. **Parking:** At the pub with permission. Alternatively, park around the
green or by the roadside in Dry Doddington.

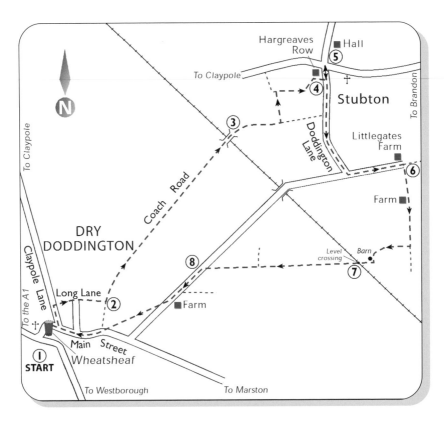

Introduction

Dry Doddington's leaning spire is a landmark visible from miles around and, conversely, astonishingly wide views can be enjoyed from the church – the Trent Valley, the Vale of Belvoir and Lincoln Cathedral can all be seen. The walk is characterised by fine views and a sense of peace and solitude, where the only sounds are those of trees and tractors – oh, and trains; high-speed trains hurtle past on the main GNER line, twice crossed during your journey.

The Wheatsheaf Inn

There can be few more appealing settings for a country inn than Dry Doddington, where the Wheatsheaf looks across the lane to the leaning church crowning the green. The inn itself is a largely 16th-century building, though part of it is said to have been a cow byre in the 13th century. Newly painted outside with a fresh ochre colour wash, the interior is also tastefully decorated, with cream and red walls and lots of wood on show. The meals are all of a very high quality, with specials each day and roast lunches on Sundays. Lighter snacks such as baguettes are also available. A range of real ales includes 'Doddington's Delight', brewed exclusively for the inn by Tom Woods. Opening times are 12 noon to 2.30 pm (4 pm on Sundays) and 5.30 pm to 11 pm (7 pm to 10.30 pm on Sundays). Food is served from 12 noon to 2 pm (3 pm on Sundays) and 6 pm to 9.30 pm – no meals are available on Sunday evenings. The inn may be closed on Mondays during the winter. Telephone: 01400 281458.

THE WALK

From the Wheatsheaf, stroll past the church and into the village. Turn left from **Main Street** into **Claypole Lane** and, just 100 yards along here, turn right onto a signed grassy path known as **Long Lane**. Despite a variety of terrains Long Lane continues unerringly in the same direction until it terminates at a firm stony track, onto which you turn left.

This delightful broad lane is the old coach road to **Stubton** and does not deviate for more than a mile, until it has bridged the main GNER track linking London with the north. Enclosed at first by tall hedges speckled with blackberries, bright red hawthorn, elderberries and blackthorn sloes, the lane rises gradually as it modifies to an open grassy track. From here the views to the elegant spires of **Claypole** and **Newark**, as well as the villages strung along the **Lincoln Cliff**, are exhilarating.

Beyond the sturdy brick railway bridge the footpath continues along the borders of two more fields, until the hedge on your right ends and wires cross overhead. At this point turn left to follow another hedge on your right until a gap ushers you to the right onto a fresh field edge path. If you reach a stile leading into woodland you have missed the gap. Along your new path a clear stile on the left soon directs you diagonally across the corner of a meadow to exit via another stile.

In front of you now stands **Hargreaves Row**, an attractive terrace of low cottages, and your route is along the narrow pathway in front of them, encountering three gates before finding yourself on **Doddington Lane**, now in the village of **Stubton**. Several buildings in Stubton warrant an inspection, including a small brick manor, the Victorian old rectory and the Georgian church. The Hall, until recently a school, stands currently disused.

Drive and Stroll

5

Begin the return journey by retracing your route along **Doddington Lane**, this time continuing for ½ mile until you see a sign for Littlegates Nursery at a junction. Do not be enticed by a parallel footpath shown on OS maps – redevelopment in Stubton seems to have obliterated all trace of it. Turn left at the junction and walk along the lawn-fringed lane as far as **Littlegates Farm**, from where a gravel track leads between the fields on your right.

6

Along here pass a yard flanked by cowsheds on the right and a long narrow lake on the left before arriving at a clear 'Public Bridleway' sign. Turn right here onto another track, which passes two more barns as it twists left then right before rising to a level crossing. Cross this with great care.

7

Beyond the railway the bridleway leads west for 1 mile until it reaches the road linking **Stubton** with **Dry Doddington**. Where this track briefly upgrades from grass to a firmer surface do not follow the improved track when it wheels to the right.

8

Turning left onto the road all eyes are now on Doddington's leaning spire on the horizon ahead. As you pass a huge farm on the left, a signed footpath cuts across the arable field on your right towards the point in **Doddington** where the coach road and **Main Street** meet. If this path is overgrown, simply remain on the road, turning right when you reach the T-junction. A short distance from here is the church and the **Wheatsheaf** inn from where you started out.

Places of Interest Nearby

Belton House, 8 miles south-east of Dry Doddington, has been the ancestral home of the Brownlows for many generations. Sumptuous rooms, Grinling Gibbons' wood-carvings and magnificent gardens can be found here. Telephone: 01476 566116.

In the opposite direction, **Newark** has retained its castle and impressive market square. Boat trips can be taken along the Trent or you can visit the Air Museum's award-winning collection of 70 aircraft. Telephone Newark Tourist Information Office for details: 01636 655765.

8 Coningsby and Tattershall Castle

The battlement walkway of Tattershall Castle is 100 ft high.

The Walk 3 miles
Terrain A level walk on firm tracks and metalled surfaces.
Map OS Explorer 261 Boston or Landranger 122 Skegness and Horncastle
(GR 215575)

How to get there

Tattershall and Coningsby cannot be missed, midway between Horncastle and Sleaford on the A153. (The Lea Gate Inn is just north of Coningsby on the B1192, which branches from the A153 and is signed for Boston.)
Parking: You should be able to park around the village green. If not, use the nearby car park for the castle.

Drive and Stroll

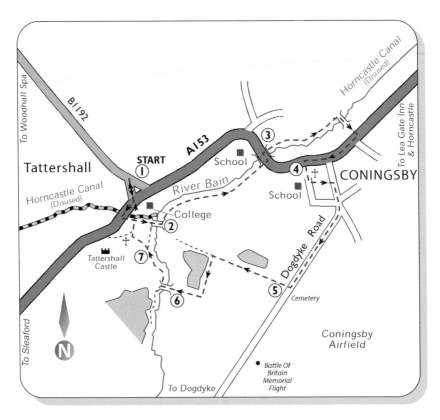

Introduction

If you have time and energy, Lincolnshire offers no greater thrill than the ascent of the brick keep of Tattershall Castle. From the battlement walkway, a hundred feet high, the lands below are spread out like a map, all points from the cathedral in Lincoln to the 'Stump' in Boston being well seen. Coningsby's claim to fame is as the home of the Battle of Britain Memorial Flight – at weekends you may be fortunate enough to experience the spectacle and thunderous noise of the mighty Lancaster taking to the skies. This walk is based upon the River Bain which divides the two villages, and which also forms part of the disused Horncastle Canal.

The Lea Gate Inn

This award-winning hostelry is a traditional inn offering excellent meals served in delightful surroundings. Low beams, real fires and an assortment of settles and pews give the bars an intimate feel, while a stylish new restaurant provides larger groups and longer legs with more spacious accommodation. Low whitewashed walls around the front entrance contrast with the lofty brick gables viewed from the large courtyard to the rear. The meals range from pies and steaks to tasty daily specials such as beef Wellington or fillet of lamb Dauphinois. Less hearty choices (for example, a selection of paninis), Sunday roasts and good vegetarian options are all available – portions are generous and everything is freshly cooked and temptingly presented. The Lea Gate is open from 12 noon to 2.30 pm and from 6 pm to 11 pm, while meals are served from 12 noon to 1.45 pm and from 6.30 pm to 8.45 pm. Winter opening times may vary. Telephone: 01526 342370.

There are, of course, many other pubs and cafés in Coningsby and Tattershall.

THE WALK

Tattershall's leafy village green served as a market square in medieval times – as witnessed by the 15th-century buttercross. Interesting features abound on and around the green, but hidden to the south is the most fascinating – the brick shell of **Ralph Cromwell's** college. Having sought out this relic, you should proceed south along the main A153 as far as the bridge over the disused **Horncastle Canal**. Turn left on the far side of the bridge onto a canal bank footpath which you follow as far as the **River Bain**. Do not be tempted by another path crossing yours and leading to the castle – this will later form the climax of your walk.

Across a railed footbridge, turn left onto the delightful mown bank-top path, the River Bain doubling as the canal at this point. After an enjoyable ½ mile the path returns you to the main road. Cross the road and river together and, via a kissing gate, resume in the same direction, now on the Bain's other bank.

The grass in this pasture is cropped short by a herd of cows who fraternise obliviously with the ducks by the water. Through the greenery on the far bank can be seen the gardens of inns and houses and, at the next kissing gate, the river is crossed by a footbridge and the main road in **Coningsby** is reached via a narrow passage running along-side one of these inns. Turn right and follow the road as far as **St Michael's church**. Enter the churchyard and pass through the arches directly beneath the church tower.

Drive and Stroll

Market Place, Tattershall.

As well as its unusual open tower archways, Coningsby's church boasts a unique one-handed clock – at 16½ ft in diameter the largest such clock face in the world.

 ④

The path weaves through the churchyard and exits via another narrow passageway on the far side, beyond which is a small roundabout by a school. Here turn left into a further passageway then right at the road. Continue over the mini-roundabout into **Dogdyke Road**, which leads you out of Coningsby until the residences on the left give way to the forbidding fence of the RAF base.

The pride of Lincolnshire's extensive aviation heritage is the Battle of Britain Memorial Flight housed at RAF Coningsby. But these aircraft are no museum pieces – they are all still flying and can regularly be spotted on their way to summer air shows. The Flight consists of a Dakota, five Spitfires, two Hurricanes and, of course, the majestic Lancaster, one of only two still airworthy.

 ⑤

When you spot a small cemetery on the left, turn right onto a gated track, indicated as a footpath to the castle. Splendid views of Tattershall's mighty castle keep and church tower now unfold. As you pass an attractive tree-fringed fishing lake on your right a fine view of **Coningsby church** can also be enjoyed. Turn left when another track crosses yours to follow the perimeter of a larger lake on your right. The grassy track, initially shaded by overhead foliage, traces the edge of the lake for two of its sides. On hot summer days groups of people may even be seen splashing about in the water – whether I recommend that you do the same is another matter.

 ⑥

From the lake the track returns you to the River Bain, which you cross by means of the sturdy iron bridge. The droning noise that may be heard at this point is not that of veteran aircraft but jet skis skimming over the surface of the nearby lakes of **Tattershall Leisure Park**, converted from former gravel pits. Turn right onto the grassy riverbank footpath. The fishponds of the castle formerly occupied the fields on your left. Once level with the church you will spot a pathway shooting across the narrow field on your left towards the churchyard.

 ⑦

If time does not permit a tour of the castle, step into the meadow next to the churchyard, colonised by rabbits and a multitude of colourful wild flowers. From here the castle may be spectacularly viewed across its deep walled moat. Having passed between the cathedral-like church and a bowling green, continue to the right of Cromwell's low brick bedehouses. The footpath now takes you over a driveway, past the car park and across your outward route and the canal. Finally you find yourself back on the main road in the heart of **Tattershall**. Now it's on to the castle to crown the day's outing with an ascent of the mighty medieval keep and the stunning panoramic views from the summit, before returning to your car and taking the short drive to the **Lea Gate Inn**.

Tattershall Castle was erected in 1440 by Ralph Cromwell, Lord High Treasurer of England. The castle fell into disrepair over the ensuing centuries but in 1911 Lord Curzon purchased and restored the magnificent keep, though the surrounding buildings have all but vanished. Cromwell's wealth was also responsible for the huge parish church, the bedehouses, the college and the market place.

Places of Interest Nearby

Woodhall Spa is a fascinating place to visit. Here you will find an open-air swimming pool, the 'Kinema in the Woods' and Dambusters' memorabilia at Petwood House, now a hotel. The **Cottage Museum** doubles as a Tourist Information Centre. Telephone: 01526 353775.

9 | Sibsey Trader Windmill

Sibsey Trader Mill and teashop.

The Walk 5 miles
Terrain A level walk from start to finish.
Map OS Explorer 261 Boston or Landranger 122 Skegness and Horncastle
(GR 354507)

How to get there

Sibsey is on the A16, 5 miles north of Boston. Heading north from Boston,
turn right into Station Road then left at the bowling green into the unnamed
road running past the church. **Parking:** Because there is very little parking at
the windmill, park near to the church in Sibsey and begin the walk from
there.

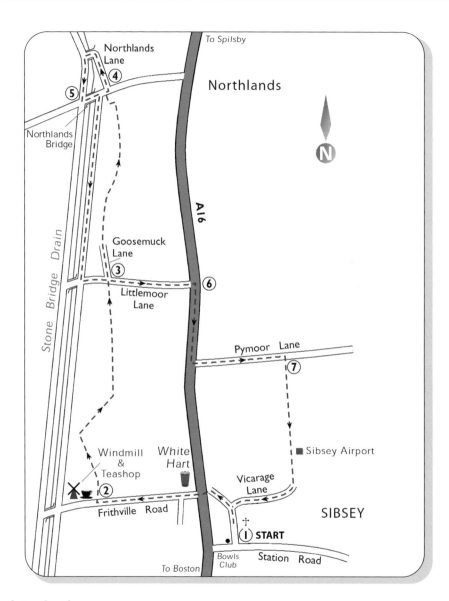

To Spilsby

Northlands Lane

④

⑤

Northlands

N

Northlands Bridge

A16

Stone Bridge Drain

Goosemuck Lane

③

⑥

Littlemoor Lane

Pymoor Lane

⑦

Windmill & Teashop

White Hart

Sibsey Airport

②

Vicarage Lane

Frithville Road

SIBSEY

① START

Bowls Club

Station Road

To Boston

Introduction

Driving through the Fens to the north of Boston the six-sailed Trader Windmill at Sibsey in full turning motion is an arresting sight and, if curiosity compels you to take a closer look, you will find a delightful tea room below the mill. A walk from the typical fenland 'galleon' of the church in the village takes in a visit to the windmill and teashop, as well as a stretch of the Stone Bridge Drain riverbank. The paths off-road are peaceful and rarely walked – this is not normally thought of as walking country – but the way is well signed and the views across the Fens towards the distant Wolds outstanding.

The Windmill Tearoom

What a wonderful way to take your afternoon tea – sitting outside the tiny tea room watching the sails of the Trader Windmill turning and creaking above your head! The bread for the sandwiches and the delicious cakes are all made from flour ground by the mill, naturally, and light meals such as jacket potatoes, salads and home-made soups are also available. Open from Easter until the end of October the tea room's opening times are from 10 am to 6 pm on Tuesdays and Saturdays, and from 11 am to 6 pm on Sundays. It may also open on Saturdays in winter. Telephone: 01205 750036.

The White Hart in Sibsey serves bar meals every day except Monday.

THE WALK

Head north from Sibsey's church and follow the road when it pivots left until you reach the busy A16 ahead. There is a pub, the **White Hart**, and a general store on the opposite block. Cross carefully and proceed along **Frithville Road**. As you clear the built-up area you are suddenly confronted by a stunning view of the towering **Trader Windmill**. Reaching the track leading to the windmill, you will see a sign made from a miniature replica of the mill, and the teashop at the foot of the tower is just a short stroll away.

Behind the teashop is a stile leading you onto a pathway through two arable fields. The path through the third field kisses the hedge, crosses a footbridge and heads half-right across the field once more, aiming for a marker at the corner of the next hedge. Now follow the clear footpath by the hedge over a quick succession of stiles and footbridges until finally a grassy path through the corn takes you to the houses on **Littlemoor Lane** – pass between the buildings to reach the lane itself.

Cross and walk up the short lane directly opposite you, **Goosemuck Lane**, at the end of which the footpath continues to the right of the hedge in front of you. The route for the next ½ mile crosses a series of bridges, fields, gates, drives, lawns and hedges too numerous to list. But the path is well signed and, by simply following the stiles, you will arrive in one last pasture behind the houses in **Northlands**. The exit from here is via a gate to the left of the houses.

Now turn right along the road, then left into **Northlands Lane**. At the end of this lane the elegant wooden footbridge spanning the **Stone Bridge Drain** marks the furthest extent of the walk. Having crossed, turn left and set off along the Drain's banktop road, peering through the hawthorn to the lily pads covering the water's surface, rippled by the taut lines of anglers.

Reaching the handsome brick arch of **Northlands Bridge**, cross the Drain again and continue along its eastern bank, passing the houses whose gardens you crossed earlier. Turn left when you reach **Littlemoor Lane** and walk its entire length.

Turn right when you arrive at the A16 and, when you spot Sibsey's village sign, turn left into **Pymoor Lane**. Along here you will spot Sibsey's other windmill to your right, tower and white cap neatly maintained but otherwise idle. On the distant horizon to your left can be seen the hills of the Lincolnshire Wolds.

When the lane bends gently left, turn right onto a clear but unsigned farmtrack known as **Green Lane**. This broad track leads you all the way to **Vicarage Lane** in Sibsey. On the way it passes a puzzling area named on some maps as Sibsey airport, a preposterous title for what is merely a grassy landing strip by a shed! At a farm turn right into **Vicarage Lane**, follow this past a number of interesting old houses and make your way back to your starting point near the church in **Sibsey**.

Places of Interest Nearby

If windmills are your passion, **Maud Foster windmill** in Boston is another mill restored to fully working condition; also another fine teashop and the chance to purchase home-ground flour. Telephone: 01205 352188.

Boston boasts numerous other attractions including the 288 ft high 'Stump', a marina from where boat trips along the river depart, and an important nature reserve at the Boston Wash Banks.

10 Halton Holegate and the Steepings

The River Lymm, Halton Holegate.

The Walk 5 miles
Terrain Some gentle hills, otherwise flat.
Map OS Explorer 274 Skegness, Alford and Spilsby or Landranger 122 Skegness and Horncastle (GR 417652)

How to get there

Halton Holegate is located 2 miles east of Spilsby on the B1195. The Bell cannot be missed at the side of the road. **Parking:** At the Bell, with permission. Otherwise you will find roadside parking along Station Road or Northorpe Road in Halton Holegate (see sketch map).

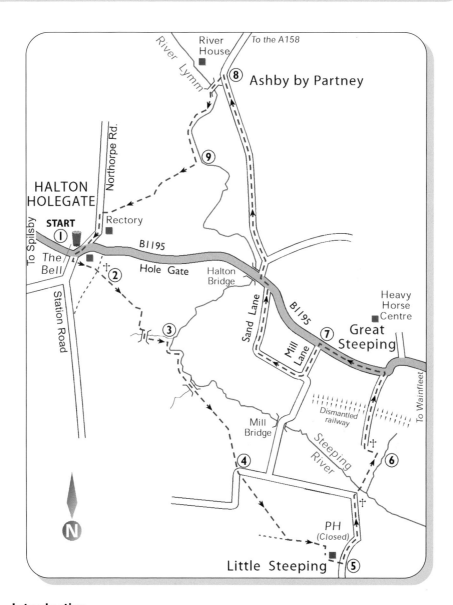

Introduction

Where wold meets marsh meets fen, east of Spilsby, quiet crooked lanes link the hidden, unspoilt villages of these parts. Your walk touches four of these ancient settlements. Between the villages meanders the River Lymm, famous as Tennyson's 'Brook', until it reaches the point where, re-aligned by the hand of man, it heads straight for the Wash as the Steeping River. The Lymm is twice followed and twice crossed on your route, which also introduces you to a team of horses enjoying their well-earned retirement.

The Bell

It is almost impossible to pass the Bell in Halton Holegate and gaze at the patrons enjoying their refreshment at the roadside tables without being enticed into their company. You should not try to resist. This most splendid setting by the tree-lined road has a long-established history of good food and real ales. It was used as their local by the 207 Squadron airmen from RAF Spilsby during the war. Tasty homely food is served here, with daily specials, lighter snacks and Sunday roasts added to the choices. The Bell is open from 12 noon to 3 pm and from 7 pm to 11 pm every day. Meals are available from 12 noon to 2.30 pm and from 7 pm to 10 pm. Telephone: 01790 753242.

THE WALK

Station Road leads south from the B1195 in Halton Holegate. Just past the manor on the corner, a narrow footpath on the left leads to a stile and into a field of cows. The path across here aims for the corner of the hedge ahead, but first make a diversion to the adjacent church.

Thomas Clay was churchwarden here in the mid 1600s and lived in a hut across the fields. Clay's dying wish that his coffin be carried across these beloved fields to the church was ignored and the road used instead. On the eve of his funeral a light was seen to cross the fields from his hut and since then it is said that if Clay's Light appears by a villager's house, then their death is imminent.

From the hedge the route continues across the pasture in a more diagonal direction to leave via another hedgerow stile. Now turn right and follow the zigzag border of the field as far as a small footbridge. Cross and continue along the other side of the hedge to the **River Lymm**.

Turn right again to accompany the playful river as it gurgles below the trees until you reach a footbridge over a lesser stream. From here the right of way leaves the delightful riverside setting and slants gently across the large field towards a group of tall trees in the corner. Beneath the trees is a smaller field which you cross in the same direction and exit via a stile. The short track you now find yourself on takes you as far as a sharp bend on an open lane.

The churchyard of All Saints' church in Great Steeping is a delight in springtime.

⇗ ④

From here your route is diagonally across the fields ahead, once more in exactly the same direction. The clear path slants through two fields to a railed footbridge, on the other side of which you turn left to pursue a hedged path along the edge of an arable field. Pivot right at the end of the field then left when you spot a broad grassy lane.

⇗ ⑤

At the end of here lies the sleepy village of **Little Steeping**. The walk continues along the lane to the left, though a brief exploration of the village in the other direction would embrace the village shop but, alas, not the public house, currently

deserted. Reaching another lofty church tower, somewhat adrift from the rest of the village, leave the lane, cross the narrow pasture and climb the levee ahead. Here the Lymm matures into the broader **Steeping River**, which you cross by means of the substantial footbridge. This is an enchanting spot, where the cows ambling through the pasture, the lazy Steeping and the trees waving in the churchyard all meet. Now stride away from the river, following the bank of a narrower watercourse until you spot a footpath heading across the pasture on your left. This takes you into the grounds of **All Saints' church** in Great Steeping, restored in 1908 but now redundant. What a sight is this churchyard in springtime, when daffodils, primroses and dandelions form a dazzling display of yellows.

Drive and Stroll

6

Leave the churchyard and begin a lengthy section of road walking. The leafy lane from the church crosses the former trackbed of the railway to Spilsby and enters **Great Steeping**. At the main B1195 cross and proceed to the left. A short distance in the opposite direction you would find the entrance to the **Heavy Horse Centre**.

The Northcote Heavy Horse Centre is a sanctuary for retired horses, where visitors are encouraged to help with some of the tasks and befriend some of the tallest horses alive. Until his death in 2001, famous resident Goliath held the world record at about 78 inches tall.

7

Continuing with the walk, a pleasant alternative to the busy road between here and Halton Bridge is to divert left when you reach **Mill Lane**, branching right into Sand Lane before returning to the main road near to the bridge. Just in front of the bridge turn right, then immediately left (both signed 'Ashby by Partney'). After half a mile, a sharp right-hand bend announces your entry into **Ashby by Partney**.

8

Retracing your steps along Ashby's main lane, do not follow the bend to the left but continue straight ahead along a narrow passage, over a stile and on to the **River Lymm**. Here the path renews its acquaintance with the meandering river, which it follows for some distance as it winds between these hilly pastures.

9

Too soon you reach a gateway where a stile on the right takes you into a larger pasture. Climb away from the river in a diagonal direction and locate carefully a stile silhouetted in a gap between the tall trees ahead. A more obvious path through the corn in the next field now guides you to **Northorpe Road** in Halton Holegate. Turning left here, you pass a succession of fine brick buildings, of which the rectory is the most splendid. When the lane pivots to the right, the **Bell** comes once more into view, and your adventure is completed.

Places of Interest Nearby

The town of **Spilsby**, famous as the birthplace of Arctic explorer Sir John Franklin, still holds a market each Monday.

In Skegness, the **Church Farm Museum** is an open-air recreation of Lincolnshire's rural buildings and lifestyles. Telephone: 01754 766658.

11 Hagworthingham and Bag Enderby

A beautiful view of the Wolds near Hagworthingham.

The Walk 4½ miles
Terrain This is a fairly hilly walk.
Map OS Explorer 273 Lincolnshire Wolds South or Landranger 122 Skegness and Horncastle (GR 345696)

How to get there

Hagworthingham straddles the A158 6 miles east of Horncastle. **Parking:** In one of several bays along the main road in Hagworthingham or turn into the village and seek a sensible roadside spot there.

Drive and Stroll

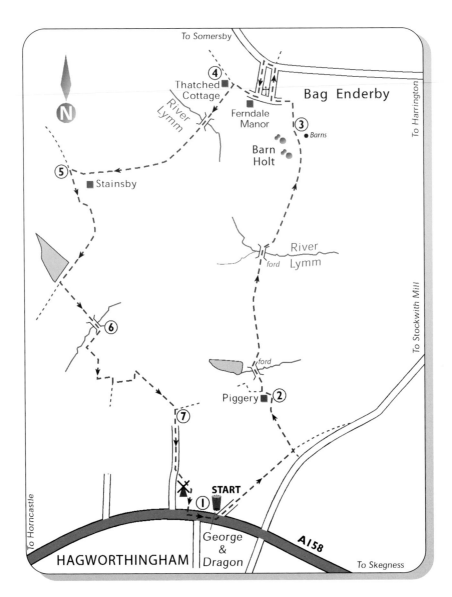

Introduction

The hills and valleys, the streams and the villages you will discover on this challenging walk will be forever famous as the homeland of Lincolnshire's greatest poet, Alfred Lord Tennyson. As you make your way through this hilly countryside, so typical of the Wolds, you are never far from a link with the Victorian Poet Laureate. Glorious hilltop views, secluded leafy hollows, playful streams and churches rich in historical heritage – little wonder that he drew such inspiration from these surroundings.

The George & Dragon

A hearty Wolds walk requires a hearty meal to accompany it, and the George & Dragon in Hagworthingham is the place to provide this. Resplendent in its dazzling coat of white paint, this handsome inn consists of three or four charming dining alcoves, although you may prefer to sit in the conservatory or outside on the spacious lawn. All food served here is locally sourced and freshly prepared to order and, in addition to the main menu, you can choose from lists of lighter snacks and special dishes. Woodland chicken in a bacon, mushroom and cream sauce and the fisherman's medley (battered cod, haddock, salmon and plaice) are two favourites, and the pasta dishes are also very popular – especially the tagliatelle carbonara.

Opening times are from 12 noon to 3 pm and from 5 pm to 11 pm (Friday to Sunday 12 noon to 11 pm). Meals can be ordered from 12 noon to 2 pm and from 5 pm to 9 pm (Friday to Sunday 12 noon to 9 pm). Telephone 01507 588255.

If the George & Dragon is not open, there is a good café on the main road in Hagworthingham.

THE WALK

From the **George & Dragon** stride out along the lane running away from the road. Past the last house on the left the route continues along a pleasant grassy path bisecting the cornfields ahead. Cross a stile and maintain your direction through a field, observing the views beginning to unfold over the **Lymm valley**. Leave via another stile, and go left along the surfaced lane and pass the piggery, beyond which the lane downgrades to a farm track.

The next mile is an absolute delight as the switchback track alternately rises to airy hilltop viewpoints and tumbles to leafy glades, where fords and footbridges cross babbling streams – one of which is Tennyson's 'Brook'.

Alfred Lord Tennyson was born in 1809 and became Poet Laureate in 1892. This walk's list of features claiming a link with Tennyson is long. The twice-crossed River Lymm is believed to be 'The Brook' in the poem of that name, and flows to nearby Stockwith, whose mill is that

Drive and Stroll

The George and Dragon, Hagworthingham.

of 'The Miller's Daughter'. Past Stockwith is Harrington Hall, visible from the walk and the location of the garden that inspired 'Maud'. The rectory in the next village of Somersby is, of course, the poet's birthplace. Somersby's church contains a bronze bust of Tennyson and his father's tombstone can be found in the graveyard.

 ③

Past **Barn Holt**, where colossal beeches face a group of flailing barns built of bright brick, the track turns to enter the peaceful village of **Bag Enderby**. Your route is straight past the church and out of the village without altering your direction. More interesting, however, is to turn right and execute a circuit of the village's

tree-lined lanes centred around an open green. Several interesting buildings are seen, including a fine example of a mud and stud cottage, in addition to the most twisted and sculpted tree stump, likened to any number of animals but actually resembling none. Now pass **Ferndale Manor** and leave Bag Enderby.

The unspoilt greenstone church in Bag Enderby looks much as it did in 1407 when it was founded by the de Enderby family. Among its treasures is an octagonal font from the same period with exquisite stone carvings. Tennyson's father was rector here from 1806 until his death in 1831.

④

At a thatched cottage, turn left to follow

the track downhill – unless your literary curiosity tempts you in the opposite direction to Tennyson's birthplace in Somersby. Continue through **Paradise Holt** to arrive back at the **River Lymm**, which you cross by means of a hidden footbridge to your left, not by the wider bridge in front of you. Now seek a yellow waymarker from which a path accompanies a ditch on its right as far as the hedge ahead. Turn left along the hedge then plunge into a dark plantation on your right. Emerge from the trees and continue along the hedgerow to a farm track. The track leads you up the hill and into a farming hamlet named **Stainsby**.

 ⑤

Turn left when you reach the metalled track and remain on this new course until you arrive at a man-made lake on the right. Here look to your left to spot another waymarker directing you along a broad hedgerow path, which terminates in the very corner of this field.

 ⑥

A footbridge now crosses a stream, on the other side of which a footpath to the right traces the winding perimeter of a field until it reaches a track. Turn right onto the track then immediately left to follow another field border as far as a stile and footbridge overlooking a deep combe. Savour these steps for they provide memorable views across the Wolds to take away with you. Beyond here the path doubles back diagonally across the next arable field to arrive at **Deep Lane** onto which you turn right.

 ⑦

As you climb through a tunnel of overhead foliage notice the cutting hewn through the exposed Spilsby sandstone. At a clear public footpath sign on your left the route slants through the field, targeting the corner of the outbuildings by a windmill tower, derelict and covered in creepers. From here a short enclosed path leads between the houses to the main road in **Hagworthingham**, and the **George & Dragon** is just a short stroll to the left.

Places of Interest Nearby

Some 3 miles south of Hagworthingham are the ruins of **Bolingbroke Castle**, birthplace of Henry IV and casualty of much Civil War strife.

The **Lincolnshire Aviation Heritage Centre** at nearby East Kirkby houses a Lancaster bomber and Barnes Wallis's original bouncing bomb. Telephone: 01790 763207.

12 Bilsby and Alford

Visitors may ascend the six floors of the five-sailed windmill, Alford.

The Walk 3½ miles
Terrain Quiet roads and field walking but all gradients are very gentle.
Map OS Explorer 274 Skegness, Alford and Spilsby or Landranger 122 Skegness and Horncastle (GR 470765)

How to get there

From Ulceby Cross, 10 miles south-east of Louth on the A16, turn left onto the A1104 and drive through Alford. As you leave the town, the A1111 (the Bilsby road) branches right and Bilsby is a mile along here. **Parking:** There is limited parking at the Three Tuns pub for patrons, but roadside parking can be found on Thurlby Road or Sutton Road in Bilsby.

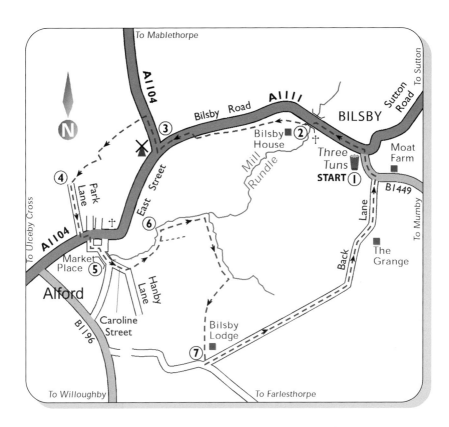

Introduction

Alford is a delightful market town, sheltering below the Wolds slopes yet only 6 miles from the North Sea coast. Here, narrow streets lined with Georgian shops and houses open out into two spacious market squares. You will also find a pottery, a folk museum and a craft market here. Your stroll approaches the town from the neighbouring village of Bilsby, taking in one of Lincolnshire's best preserved windmills and returning via a streamside path known as the Mill Rundle Walk.

Drive and Stroll

The Three Tuns

Each summer, hordes pass this old white pub in Bilsby on their journey to the bustling coastal resorts – they might not speed by if they knew what they were missing. The Three Tuns has won awards for its food and the compact interior is gradually being transformed into an elegant dining area. The food is all freshly prepared by the owners and the menu changes regularly and seasonally – favourites such as liver and onions and steak casserole take on an extra flavour here. Less hearty snacks, Sunday roasts and vegetarian options are all available and the beers include Boddington's and Flowers IPA. The Three Tuns is open from 12 noon to 2 pm (Sunday 3 pm) and from 7 pm to 11 pm (Sunday 10.30 pm). Food is available until 8.30pm. Telephone 01507 462297 The inn does not open on Mondays or at lunchtime on Tuesdays in winter. Telephone 01507 462297.

The tea room at the five-sailed windmill also serves excellent food, as does the Half Moon in Alford.

THE WALK

① From the centre of **Bilsby**, where the inn and the shell of a windmill of unusual profile face each other, set off west towards **Alford** along the main A1111. A number of splendid houses are situated around Bilsby and the rectory on your right is the first. Enter the churchyard of **Holy Trinity church** opposite here and leave via the far gate.

② At this point a signed footpath leads through a kissing gate and between the tall trees to a footbridge. Now in the parkland surrounding **Bilsby House**, continue along the edge of the wood, cross the driveway and go over a stile. The footpath now continues through three pastures linked by stiles and taking you as far as a rough track. The right of way here remains tight to the main road, until it joins the road itself where an alternative field path shoots left towards Alford. When the shaded road you are on terminates, turn right onto **East Street**. From behind the trees the spectacular tower of **Alford's windmill** now looms dramatically – even when the sails are not turning.

Alford's five-sailed windmill – properly named Hoyle's Mill – is almost 200 years old and rises to a height of 95 feet. The sails and cap were renewed in 1978 and the mill now produces organic stone-ground flours on a daily basis. Visitors may ascend the six floors of the tarred tower, and the views from the white-railed balcony are glorious.

③ Continue along East Street away from Alford and locate a sign on the left

The Market Place at Alford.

reading 'Public footpath to Alford'. From here a mown path runs along the edge of the field. As your gaze remains drawn to the windmill, do not forget to turn and admire the views towards the hills of the nearby **Wolds**. Keeping the hedgerow on your left at all times, the way encounters a short tunnel of overhead branches and two metal kissing gates before it returns you to residential Alford, now at the end of **Park Lane**.

Follow Park Lane to Alford's busy main street (the A1104) and execute a sharp left-right movement to find

yourself in the delightful **Market Place**. There is much of interest in Alford's hub. Tall handsome buildings line the Market Place, a Victorian pump and a set of stocks can be seen, and a visit to **Saint Wilfrid's church** should not be missed.

As its name suggests, Alford's origins are as a river crossing point. When the stream was re-channelled for drainage purposes, it became known as the Wold Grift and later the Mill Rundle. Alford's prosperity as a market town lasted until the late 20th century, with the annual bull fair continuing until 1972 and the cattle market not closed until 1987. Of several thatched properties

Drive and Stroll

along the main street, by far the most attractive is the H-shaped Manor House, newly renovated and housing the Tourist Information Centre and a folk museum.

At the southern end of the Market Place you will see **Caroline Street** leading off to the left. Along here continue straight ahead onto a track when the road angles right into **Hanby Lane** – the sign informs you that you are now following the **Mill Rundle Walk**. Branch left at a meeting of tracks and enter an unkempt meadow, keeping close to the tall trees on the left.

Reaching the **Mill Rundle** itself, follow it to the right along a pleasant footpath until progress is barred by another stream. Again turn right and follow this stream along a clear path until

you arrive at a gate. Beyond here the right of way continues by the waterside but now in altogether more spacious pastures – rabbits, moorhens and inquisitive cows are your company here. Three stiles later you reach tarmac once again, at **Bilsby Lodge**.

Turn left at the junction (signed 'Bilsby') and march briskly along the arrow-straight lane ahead of you. When the lane begins to meander, pass an imposing brick grange and the extraordinary hedgerow topiary of a white cottage to re-enter **Bilsby**. Turn left at the renovated dairy – although an inspection of the ancient gabled **Moat Farm** on the far side of **Thurlby Road** is most worthwhile More interesting old brick houses, including a low thatch, now punctuate your return journey along Thurlby Road to the **Three Tuns** pub.

Places of Interest Nearby

Visits to Alford's **five-sailed windmill** and **thatched folk museum** must take pride of place, naturally. On the nearby coast, seal sanctuaries have been established at both **Mablethorpe** (telephone 01507 473346) and **Skegness** (01754 764345).

13 | South Thoresby, Belleau and Aby

The dovecote at Belleau was built in the 16th century.

The Walk 4 miles
Terrain Road walking and country paths, with a few gentle inclines.
Map OS Explorer 274 Skegness, Alford and Spilsby or Landranger 122 Skegness and Horncastle (GR 402768)

How to get there

On the A16, 8 miles south of Louth, a signed road on the left leads you straight into South Thoresby. From the opposite direction another road (on the right, naturally) does the same – but be careful not to miss the turn off left to the Vine pub and the church. **Parking:** At the pub for patrons or drive down the hill and turn right towards the church – you will be able to park by the roadside along here.

Drive and Stroll

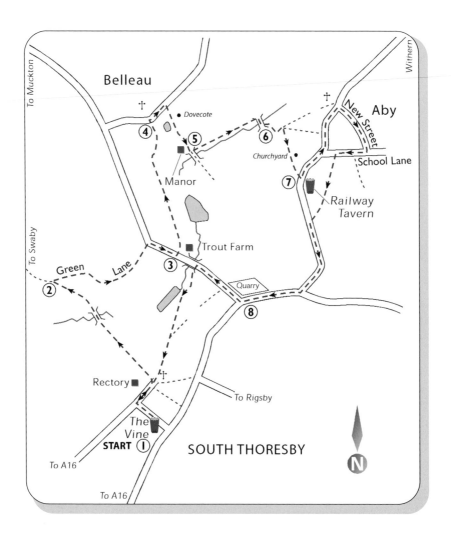

Introduction

This is a rewarding walk around the lower slopes of the Wolds to the south of Louth. Springs and streams bubble up from the chalky Wolds and set off towards the coast, and the Great Eau is one stream whose acquaintance you will continually renew. Verdant greenery is all around and herons will no doubt be seen lazily flapping through this land of wood and water. There is much of historical interest, including halls and churches – some vanished, some still standing – and a hidden wild man of former heraldic importance.

The Vine

Baskets and tubs of colourful flowers welcome you into this handsome old country inn that originally incorporated the smithy, the general store and the post office. The tiniest of bars is flanked by a cosy dining room to one side and a stylish restaurant to the other. The menu contains all the dishes and snacks you would expect but the Specials board offers a few different ideas. Try the wild boar in a port and red wine sauce or the game meatballs on red cabbage. Booking is recommended if planning your Sunday lunch here, when traditional roasts replace the usual menu. The Vine's opening times are 12 noon to 3 pm and 7 pm to 11 pm. Meals are available from 12 noon to 2 pm and from 7 pm to 9 pm – no food is served on Thursdays. Telephone: 01507 480273.

During the winter months the inn is closed on Tuesday and Thursday lunchtimes but the Railway Tavern in Aby also serves meals.

THE WALK

From your parking spot in **South Thoresby** make your way down to the Georgian church.

Several impressive houses can be seen around the village but the finest is the old rectory opposite the church. The banded brickwork and octagonal turret mark this as the vigorous design of architect S. S. Teulon. It was suggested that the skilful display of gables and chimneys was merely incorporated to tempt prospective clients. More certain is that the bricks for the Victorian rectory were salvaged from South Thoresby's hall, demolished in the 1820s.

Between church and rectory a stile takes you into a grassy field. Hug the left-hand hedgerow to reach a gurgling stream, cross the footbridge and enter a pasture. Navigational awareness is required at this point. The way is not straight ahead towards a footbridge below the trees but half-left between the marshes (stick to the raised walkways) in the direction of a clear footpath sign. Over another stile and footbridge follow the edge of the next field to the left and into a corner where woodland on both sides converges to create an apparent impasse. A clear path does cut through the undergrowth, however, and rises to emerge at a hedged bridleway named **Green Lane**.

If time permits, a stroll to the left would take you through a beautiful glacial valley to the sleepy village of **Swaby**. Otherwise follow the bridleway to the right, keeping the belt of horse chestnut, field maple and elderberry alongside. The track angles to trace a delightful crescent around an open field flanked by a belt of tall trees before arriving at a road. Turn right onto this and descend to **Belleau Bridge**.

Drive and Stroll

The route takes you by Belleau Manor estate.

③

Along here a signed footpath leads into the woods just before the old trout farm. This enchanting path narrows and crosses two streams before emerging into sunlight at a clear path through the field ahead. The first of three sturdy stiles then takes you briefly onto the grassy hillside above a water meadow, where hidden pools and springs run clear. Without losing height the other stiles take you in and out of another field. Finally, a short, shaded section returns you to a road overlooking the church in **Belleau**, a village which lives up to the meaning of its name – 'beautiful water'.

④

Stroll downhill past the church gates until you see a clear farm track leading off to the right. Halt to admire the

dovecote, then again to inspect the farm buildings converted from the manor house of the Willoughbys d'Eresby.

The octagonal brick dovecote was built in the 16th century and formed part of the estate of Belleau Manor. Only the nobility were allowed to keep pigeons until 1613, when the right was extended to commoners. The Tudor stonework around the windows of the manor can still be seen, but most striking is the mighty bearded head and bust of the 'wodewose', the wild man who was the symbol of the Willoughbys. This medieval stone relic is curiously set into a building of 1904, although illustrations exist showing it mounted above an arched gateway of the 1500s.

⑤

Beyond the farm, the track winds

towards a stream in front of which an indicated footpath crosses the cattle grid on the left. Follow the stream through this idyllic pasture until it is spanned by a wooden footbridge – do not miss the views behind you of Belleau and the hills.

Keeping to the hedge leading away from the stream, locate and cross a smaller footbridge on your left. Several paths appear to cross the next meadow – simply aim for the cultivated yew trees to your right. These surround the neat lawns of Aby's vanished church – a few mounds and gravestones are the sole remains. Leave this evocative spot via the mown track leading you to the road by the **Railway Tavern**.

From the inn, a detour left around the lanes in **Aby** is to be recommended. Past the smithy, still operational, to the converted chapel, turn right into **New Street**, where a number of interesting old cottages can be seen. Turn right at the junction with **School Lane** and pass **Glebe Cottages** on the left to locate a narrow fenced path leading you once more onto grass. Over a stile at the end of the first field regain the road via the gate on the right of the second. Now stride out to the left for half a mile along this open country road.

When you re-enter wooded surroundings turn right into the road leading back to **Belleau Bridge**, peering carefully into the deep disused quarry on the corner. Ignore the first footpath sign on your left but enter the field at the second. Sharp eyes may spot **Park Bridge** as this delightful wooded waterside path leads you below the parkland in which South Thoresby's old hall once stood. At a windpump the path angles slightly away from the waterside to climb gradually through the next two fields, separated by a stile. In the corner of the second field, you will recognise the next stile as your starting point, now back at the church in **South Thoresby**.

Places of Interest Nearby

The Great Eau flows from South Thoresby to **Claythorpe Mill**, the picturesque setting of an 18th-century waterwheel and a unique collection of unusual wildfowl. Telephone: 01507 450687.

Louth museum just 8 miles away, has been recently extended to house new exhibitions and galleries. Telephone 01507 601211.

14 Goulceby and Red Hill

The Three Horseshoes is hidden down Shoe Lane in Goulceby.

The Walk 5 miles
Terrain Firm road walking with rural paths and a few steepish climbs.
Map OS Explorers 273 Lincolnshire Wolds South and 282 Lincolnshire Wolds North, or Landranger 122 Skegness and Horncastle (GR 253790)

How to get there

Some 4 miles north of Horncastle, on the A153, a signed road forks left to Goulceby. Reaching a T-junction in the village turn left, then left again into Shoe Lane, where you will see the Three Horseshoes. **Parking:** At the pub with permission or park considerately in one of the lanes around Goulceby.

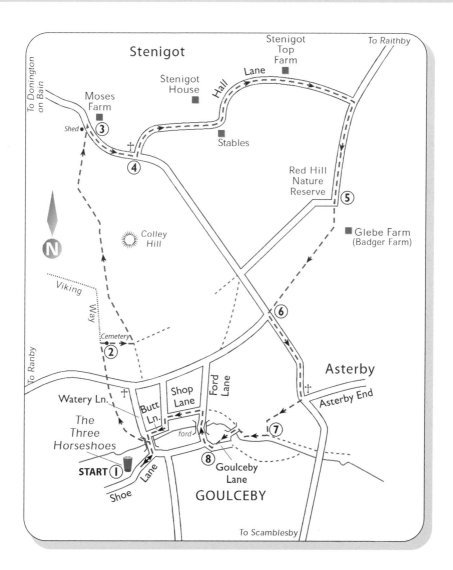

Introduction

One of the Viking Way's most popular stretches passes through the sheltered village of Goulceby in the heart of the Lincolnshire Wolds. The village has grown around a playful brook, a tributary of the River Bain and your companion for much of the walk. In contrast the route rises to the very top of the Wolds before dropping down over the ridge towards the valley once

Drive and Stroll

more. This is the Lincolnshire of hidden farming hamlets and tiny wayside churches, of secluded shaded streams and dramatic hilltop panoramas. These are the ingredients of your walk, which also features an important nature reserve and an unassuming country inn, the starting point and conclusion of your journey.

The Three Horseshoes

Hidden down Shoe Lane in Goulceby is the Three Horseshoes, an inn with no passing trade but well-known to locals, Viking Way walkers and Cadwell Park's motor racing fraternity. Here, original heavy ceiling beams and open fires conjure a welcoming atmosphere. The delicious steaks are a speciality and the Sunday roast lunches are also very popular. All tastes are catered for with snacks, sandwiches and good vegetarian options included in an extensive menu. Usual opening times apply but lunchtime opening in the winter months is restricted to Sundays. However, meals can be arranged for walking groups outside these hours. Telephone 01507 343610.

Nearby the Black Horse in Donington on Bain also serves good food, as do inns in Belchford and Hemingby.

THE WALK

Turn left out of **Shoe Lane** into **Watery Lane**, cross the stream and look out for a kissing gate on your left. On the other side of the gate a clear track rises through the meadow before veering left towards another kissing gate, beneath trees in the corner of the field. A grassy track leads from here to a third kissing gate by a road. The route now continues along the gravel track on the opposite side of the road, but first step to the right for an inspection of **All Saints' church**.

All Saints' is a small and simple but smart and beautifully-maintained church. Goulceby's old church was demolished in 1886 and the stone used to build its successor, consecrated 23 years later. Some medieval fragments were also worked into the rebuilding, including the font and some window tracery.

A short distance along the track is an overgrown cemetery, a sad and eerie spot. A mown path along the edge of this plot leads you to the next kissing gate, from where you follow an open field path as far as yet another kissing gate on your right. At this point turn left and set off along a well-defined path through the corn. Having climbed and descended **Colley Hill**, the footpath cuts through a narrow belt of coniferous trees, crosses another arable field and enters a deeper wood.

The 'patchwork' All Saints' church at Asterby.

This enchanting path, strewn with cones (perfect for your Christmas decorations), takes you as far as an attractive rolling pasture, entered via a stile and fringed by woods on all sides. The route across here follows the marker posts between two gigantic beeches towards a wooden shed – notice two particularly striking copper beeches amongst the trees ahead.

 ③

Cross the stile by the shed, turn right and set off along the lane, having first admired the brick ranges of **Moses Farm** and the bright red dogwood close by. Turn left at the junction on which Stenigot's tiny church stands.

 ④

Now on **Hall Lane**, neatly-trimmed

hedges and lawns soon develop alongside you – although **Stenigot House** itself is glimpsed only briefly through a gateway. Entering dense woodland the lane rises steeply as it snakes past the noble stable block, eventually emerging into sunlight near to the top of the hill. When the road terminates at a T-junction turn right and gradually descend to **Red Hill**.

An abandoned hillside quarry has left a brick-red gash exposed high on the steep side of Red Hill, now designated as a nature reserve. The layer of red chalk, which owes its colour to the presence of iron, is topped by a layer of white chalk. The steepness of the hillside makes it unsuitable for farming, and the result is a profusion of rare wild

Drive and Stroll

flowers, including kidney vetch and the purple-flowered pyramidal orchid. Information boards detail the natural history of the nature reserve.

 (5)

Just before the road bends sharply to plunge downhill, step into the entrance to **Badger Farm**, the site of the annual Ecofest rock festival, and carefully locate a hidden footpath between the hedges here. This rather constricted section emerges on the open hillside and continues as an untamed path between a fence and an encroaching hedge all the way to the road. A fine view of the exposed red chalk on the hillside compensates for this awkward stretch, but if preferred the road can be followed down **Red Hill** to turn left at the bottom and rejoin the route.

 (6)

The road now leads you south for ½ mile to a green island where a single sycamore indicates the way into the secluded hamlet of **Asterby**. Step between the yews to view the small patchwork church before locating a signed footpath on the other side of the road leading you across another cornfield. Reaching a beech tree, turn left onto an enclosed path taking you down to the stream, at which point you rejoin the **Viking Way**.

 (7)

Turn right along this delightful stream bank path until a track crosses your way. Continue onto the grassy path beyond this track but then turn left immediately to cross the stream via a little wooden footbridge. Carefully trace the edge of a private lawn and go over a stile into a meadow full of wild flowers in summer.

 (8)

The next stile takes you to **Goulceby Lane**, onto which you turn right, then right again when you reach **Ford Lane**. Beyond the shaded ford itself, turn left into **Shop Lane** – now shopless! Turn left at the T-junction, follow **Butt Lane** back to **Watery Lane**, then turn left to make your way back to the **Three Horseshoes**.

Places of Interest Nearby

To the south of Goulceby is the market town of **Horncastle**, once the stage for England's largest horse fair but today more well-known for the antique shops found along its narrow streets. Between Goulceby and Horncastle is **Cadwell Park**, a hilly and challenging motor racing circuit. Each August Bank Holiday tens of thousands of fans flock here for the British Superbike Championships. Telephone 01507 343248.

15 | Lincoln and the Fossdyke

The Fossdyke Navigation near Lincoln.

The Walk 4 miles
Terrain A level walk on firm grassy riverbanks, with one section of road walking.
Map OS Explorer 272 Lincoln or Landranger 121 Lincoln and Newark on Trent (GR 949724)

How to get there

Head north-west from Lincoln on the A57. Half a mile beyond the by-pass roundabout a narrow signed lane leads off to the left and the Pyewipe Inn is found at the end of this lane. **Parking:** At the Pyewipe for patrons but please ask before leaving your car whilst you walk.

Drive and Stroll

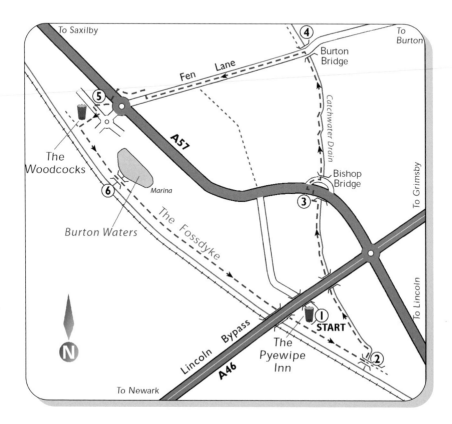

Introduction

A perfect antidote to the excesses of modern life, this route follows the line of an historic Roman canal before continuing along a more peaceful riverbank into deep rural Lincolnshire. Your return along the Fossdyke Navigation takes you past an exclusive new marina before arriving back at a long-established inn with a matchless waterside setting. Along here motorboats, narrowboats and swans cut gently through the deep water, and the whole walk is illuminated by stunning views of Lincoln's medieval skyline.

The Pyewipe Inn

This is a handsome canal-side inn at the very end of its own lane. Enjoying your meal and a refreshing drink on the terrace above the neatly mown banks of the Fossdyke, it is easy to forget that the hustle and bustle of Lincoln is only a couple of miles away. Here the mouth-watering menus are all chalked onto wallboards around the dark, low-beamed bar area. The choices rotate regularly and might include braised venison, beef and Guinness pie and fresh fish dishes. An excellent selection of real ales includes Bombardier, Timothy Taylor's Landlord and Abbot's Ale among its number. Furthermore the Pyewipe is open from 11 am to 11 pm (12 noon to 10.30 pm on Sundays) and food is served all the time until 9.30 pm. Telephone: 01522 528708.

Refreshments are also available on the walk from the Woodcocks at Burton Waters.

THE WALK

From the **Pyewipe**, set off on the concrete cycle track running along the raised bank of the **Fossdyke** in the direction of Lincoln. You quickly arrive at an interesting old bridge where a lesser watercourse unites with the Fossdyke. Admire the black and white brick arch and ornate rails of the bridge but do not cross it, opting instead for the grassy footpath on the other side of the stile on your left.

The Fossdyke Navigation is the canal cut by the Romans to link the Witham in Lincoln with the River Trent, making this one of the country's oldest canals. The canal was deepened in medieval times to allow more ambitious traffic to pass, further increasing Lincoln's prosperity and strategic importance. Today the traffic along this 12-mile waterway from Torksey to Brayford Pool in Lincoln is leisure based, and includes expensive motorboats making their way to and from the marina at Burton Waters.

Now continue along the left-hand bank of the Catchwater Drain for almost 1 mile, passing underneath Lincoln's by-pass midway and enjoying the rural nature of the surroundings so close to such a large city. The views are marvellous, and you can plan your itinerary for a visit from here – cathedral, castle and windmill are neatly arranged along the hilltop skyline. Your path, between the reeds, bulrushes and lily pads on your right and the horses in the thistly fields to your left, leads you to **Bishop Bridge**, a concrete construction displaying a surprising attention to detail and design.

Cross the road and walk left to discover the old road leading off to the right towards the original brick-built bridge. Rejoin the left-hand bank of the **Catchwater Drain** here (signed 'Burton Bridge') and continue in the shade of the overhanging trees on the far bank for $^1/_2$ mile, now in totally rural surroundings.

Drive and Stroll

4

Reaching **Burton Bridge** turn left and stroll along **Fen Lane**, deep woods on either side screening lakes created from former gravel pits. Approaching the A57 do not miss the fenced footpath on your right channelling you far enough from the busy roundabout to be able to cross safely and continue into the trees on the far side, on the course of what is clearly the original road. You have now entered an area which has been entirely redeveloped as an exclusive resort radiating from a central marina – Burton Waters.

5

The old road brings you to the gates of the **Woodcocks Inn**. Follow the road leading past these gates to the left for a short distance. Look carefully for an enclosed footpath on the right leading all the way back to the raised levee of the **Fossdyke**. At the riverbank turn left and resume your earlier bearing in the direction of Lincoln. Along here the entrance to the marina itself is spanned by a stylish green footbridge. This is the best point from which to survey the central feature of the marina, the circular tower from where the comings and goings of expensive modern boats of all sizes are controlled.

6

The banktop footpath continues behind the new houses – many boasting balcony views of the Fossdyke – towards the ring road passing overhead again. At this point the **Pyewipe Inn** comes into view once more, just a few hundred yards along the riverbank.

Places of Interest Nearby

The attractions of **Lincoln** are manifold, of course: cathedral, castle, palace, museums – the list is endless. Telephone Lincoln Tourist Information Office for details: 01522 873213.

Those seeking a more peaceful diversion might head west along the bypass to **Doddington Hall**, a spectacular Elizabethan mansion surrounded by romantic gardens. Telephone: 01522 694308.

16 | Stow Minster, Marton and the River Trent

The River Trent near Marton is followed during the walk.

The Walk 2½ miles
Terrain Some road walking combined with good tracks and paths.
Map OS Explorer 271 Newark on Trent or Landranger 121 Lincoln and Newark on Trent (GR 882820)

How to get there

The A1500 runs west from the A15, 4 miles north of Lincoln; When you reach the crossroads in Marton, turn right, then immediately left into Littleborough Lane. **Parking:** Roadside parking along the residential section of Littleborough Lane.

Drive and Stroll

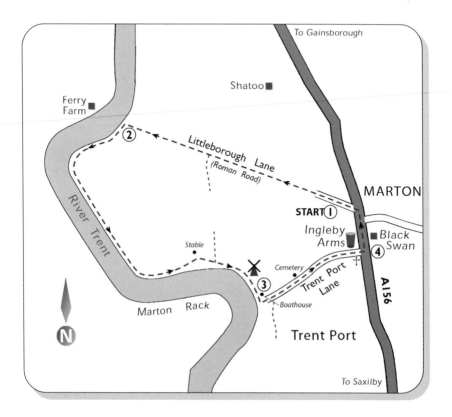

Introduction

This easy but exhilarating walk follows the course of a Roman thoroughfare and the curving bank of the mighty River Trent, offering vast views across the Trent lowlands that will linger long in your memory. The outing can be combined with a visit to an exceptional country inn at nearby Stow and a stroll around Stow Minster, a few miles to the east. This soaring medieval monument dominates the Lincolnshire countryside and is an unforgettable sight.

The Cross Keys

This pub, 2½ miles east of Marton, enjoys a proud position in the shadow of Stow Minster. Like the Minster, the original inn has been much extended and it is now a warren of dining areas. This is a very special place, more of a restaurant than a pub serving food and, as it is always popular, booking is essential at busy times. The menu and a list of specials on wallboards include dishes ranging from the favourite steak and mushroom pie to more exotic sounding choices. You might find pheasant breast with an orange, lemon and thyme stuffing or duck breast in a rhubarb and ginger sauce. There's Dennett's ice cream to follow, and all food is freshly prepared and exquisitely presented. The Cross Keys is open from 12 noon to 3 pm and from 6 pm to 11 pm. Meals are served from 12 noon to 2 pm and from 6.30 pm to 10 pm. Telephone 01427 788314.

The Ingleby Arms in Marton also serves food at certain times.

THE WALK

Head down **Littleborough Lane** which soon downgrades to a pleasant tree-lined track and, for a Roman road, seems most reluctant to take the shortest distance between any two points. Peer through gaps in the foliage on the right to spot the 'Shatoo' – or chateau – belonging to **Gate Burton Hall**. In the opposite direction the horizon is dominated by the dramatic outline of the power station across the Trent at Cottam in Nottinghamshire. The lane terminates abruptly on the banks of the **River Trent**, at the point where the ferry once carried people to and from the Roman town of **Littleborough**, now no more than a couple of farms on the opposite bank.

Set off left along the raised grassy riverbank and begin to absorb the sweeping views along the river and across the expanses on the far side. The mighty Trent traces a continual gentle arc to the left until, at a stretch known as **Marton Rack**, you feel as though you have almost turned full circle. Eventually reaching a gate just past a stable and paddock, you will see that a footpath ascends the steep bank on your left. This is not your route but from the top of the bank a high-level view back along the river and your approach can be enjoyed. Beyond the gate your path continues through an enchanted wooded stretch below the cliff.

Place of Interest Nearby

As well as a visit to Stow Minster, **Gainsborough Old Hall** is another gem. Located 5 miles north of Marton, it is a half-timbered manor house whose towering hall and splendid kitchens have changed little since the visit of Richard III in 1483. Telephone: 01427 612669.

Drive and Stroll

The Cross Keys and Minster at Stow.

The surroundings open up as you reach **Trent Port**, nowadays no more than a private jetty and slipway. Pass the boathouse and ascend the levee to your left. Now proceed away from the river along the surfaced lane ahead, passing a small cemetery and re-entering **Marton**. Turn left into the **High Street** at the junction by the church – note the conspicuous blue anchor mounted to commemorate the Millennium. The leaning tower of the church itself is a rare example of Saxon herring-bone masonry.

A number of elegant brick buildings, including the former Black Swan coaching inn, indicate Marton's erstwhile importance as a port. Soon enough you will recognise **Littleborough Lane** on your left, the end of your journey.

17 The Wolds Escarpment from Walesby

A stunning view of the Lincolnshire Wolds near Normanby le Wold.

The Walk 5 miles
Terrain A fairly challenging walk, with some stiff gradients.
Map OS Explorer 282 Lincolnshire Wolds North or Landranger 113 Grimsby (GR 132922)

How to get there

From the traffic lights in Market Rasen, take the B1203 towards Grimsby. Turn left after ½ mile at the sign for Walesby – the Walesby tea room is on the left 1½ miles from here. **Parking:** At the tea room with permission or in the nearby village hall car park.

Drive and Stroll

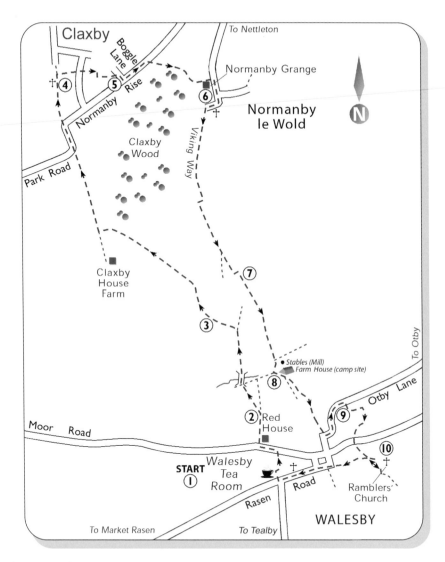

Introduction

This richly rewarding trek into the hilly Lincolnshire Wolds belies its mere 5 miles in length. As the exhilarating switchback takes you to the highest point of the Wolds, the views simply get better and better. Four churches in three villages are visited and even a vineyard is included. Much of the route follows the clear golden helmets of the Viking Way, but some navigational competence will prove useful. Walesby's charming little tea room can mark either the start or the end of your journey – indecisive walkers may even spoil themselves and make two visits!

Walesby Tea Room

The 16th-century farm building next to Walesby House has been converted into this delightful tea room. Here you can choose from such tempting snacks as smoked salmon and cream cheese sandwiches, Brie and bacon toasties and mozzarella, pesto and sun-dried tomato paninis. Cooked lunches and home made soups are available, as well as sponge puddings and a wonderful selection of cakes. Afterwards you will not want to miss the 'Maps to Treasure' room above the tea room. The maps exhibited are exquisitely detailed and show Lincolnshire as it was 100 years ago – you can order a unique reprint for any part of the county. Walesby Tea Room is open from Wednesday to Sunday between the hours of 10 am and 5 pm. Telephone: 01673 838969.

No other refreshment halts are passed en route but pubs and teashops can be found in Market Rasen and Tealby.

THE WALK

Stroll through the farmyard used as the tea room car park and locate a gateway on the right. On the other side of the gate a mown path twists clearly through the grassy meadow and leaves via a signed gravel track between the houses. Turn left when you reach the road, then right onto a track just past **Red House**, signposted for Mill House Farm. You are now on the **Viking Way** and, having cleared the hedged section of the track, broad views open up of the Wolds ahead.

Where the track forks at a 'Public Byway' sign, branch left, soon to cross a stream (nowadays bridged – the ford marked on some OS maps no longer exists) and enter an open pasture via a cattle grid. Keep close to the hedge on your left, especially when the Viking Way attempts to lure you up the open hillside. Now on a rough grass track along an elevated terrace you may enjoy far-reaching views over the hedge on your left. **Hamilton Hill** is seen protruding above **Willingham Woods** and on the distant horizon the silhouette of **Lincoln Cathedral** is discernible.

The track improves as a narrow belt of woodland develops on its right then gradually descends and veers past the corner of **Claxby Wood**. The track ends at the metalled lane leading to Claxby House Farm – turn right and follow this to **Park Road**, onto which you also turn right. At the next bend cross a stile to enter **Claxby Park** and follow the indicated permissive path along the hedge. Leave the park via another stile – this one made of iron – to find yourself in the wooded precincts of **Saint Mary's church** in Claxby.

Just past the church gate seek a narrow signed bridleway on the right which skirts a horse paddock midway before reaching a lane. At this point the earthworks of an ancient moat occupy the field to your right. Cross the lane and continue along the fence of the **Old Smithy**, at the end of which is a kissing gate and a meadow of long grass. As you follow the mown path around the meadow's perimeter, note the **Three Sisters Vineyard** on your left, planted in 2002 and claiming to be the most northerly in Europe. Carefully seek a hidden gate along the meadow's second edge, which in turn leads you along a hedged passage, across a private lawn and over another meadow, which you exit by the gate clearly defined by sky-blue gateposts.

Now in Boggle Lane turn right for a few yards then left onto **Normanby Rise**. At the point where **Claxby Wood** touches the road clear a stile to enter a steep field of grass. The path stays close to the wood as it picks a way between the grassy hillocks. The gradient is unforgiving but the views behind you reward those moments spent catching your breath. At the

end of the wood locate a stile in the hedgerow above you. Beyond the stile simply follow the stone wall of **Normanby Grange** until you arrive at a quiet lane. Turn right and stroll into **Normanby le Wold**, once more on the Viking Way.

Most of Normanby's buildings and barns tumble down the hillside into the leafy hollow on the left. But your route is straight ahead to the church, founded near to Lincolnshire's highest point and boasting excellent views of the lowlands below. The route passes the weathered tower of the church and enters the first of a series of pastures at a stile. It is a secret that perhaps should not be disclosed but the sloes gathered along here make excellent gin! Keeping the hedge on your left continue through these pastures until you eventually begin to lose height.

It is important here that you do not miss a gate taking you onto the opposite side of the hedge. The path – now along the edges of arable fields – descends rapidly for a full $1/2$ mile until a gate takes you into a small horse paddock, where the stables are converted from an original stone watermill.

Reaching a lane via a small footbridge, turn into the mown field used as a caravan site and target the metal gate in its far corner. Through here the path bisects a field of crops before joining a hedgerow leading you to a shaded lane in **Walesby**. Turn left and follow the lane left and right as it climbs the hill towards **Otby**.

Look out for a gate and a stile leading you onto a grassy track through the meadow on the right. Follow a series of green and white markers – this is 'open access' countryside and no paths are marked on your OS maps. The path is more vague through a second meadow but by keeping to the right of an impenetrable patch of gorse and hawthorn you will correctly descend to another roadside stile. From the meadow you will have admired the sturdy tower of a nearby church, and that is your next destination. Walk left along the road then clear another stile on your right. Through the next pasture the gradient is decidedly upwards. A further stile now leads you onto the rough track curving up to the redundant church

above Walesby – the **Ramblers' Church**.

All Saints' church, known as the Ramblers' church, was once surrounded by the houses of Walesby village, but over the years the exposed site was forsaken and the villagers moved down into the sheltered valley. The abandoned church was restored in the 1930s and adopted by ramblers. A unique stained-glass window shows Christ leading a group of walkers and cyclists. The annual candle – lit carol service held at the Ramblers is a memorable event.

From the church about turn and retrace your steps, this time remaining on the track and allowing it to guide you all the way back down into **Walesby**, where the tea room is on the right just past **St Mary's church**.

Places of Interest Nearby

Market Rasen is home to a friendly racecourse, some of whose meetings are held in the evening. Telephone 01673 843434 for dates and times.

The former RAF base at **Hemswell**, 12 miles west of here, has been converted to a complex of antique, craft and design centres.

18 | The Lost Villages of the Wolds

The peaceful scene near Wold Newton.

The Walk 4½ miles
Terrain Mainly firm bridleways, with a few steep inclines.
Map OS Explorer 282 Lincolnshire Wolds North or Landranger 113 Grimsby (GR 267972)

How to get there

From the A16 Louth to Grimsby road, turn west at North Thoresby. Cross the A18 (Barton Street). The start of the walk is at a sharp left-hand bend by a barrel-roofed barn. **Parking:** Although there is no recognised parking you will be able to park by the road at the start of the walk.

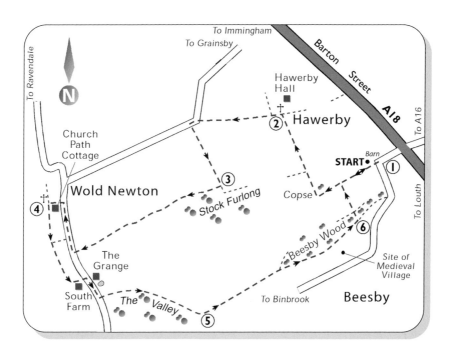

Introduction

The Lincolnshire Wolds is a designated Area of Outstanding Natural Beauty and the Wanderlust Way weaves through some of the most splendid villages and scenery these hills can offer. This route follows the Way for much of its length, enjoying dramatic views towards the Humber estuary and a secluded leafy valley section. Romantic churches and long deserted villages are among the rewards for what is a considerable amount of effort – and they say that this is the shallow slope of the Wolds! A rather special inn makes a fitting prelude or postscript to the walk.

The New Inn

This North Thoresby pub is just 2½ miles away from the start of the walk. It is reached by crossing the A18 and A16 and driving through the village to Station Road. The inn's reputation is such that booking ahead is necessary at busy times. You will find Grimsby haddock or skate on the menu and the minted lamb Henrie uses only fresh Lincolnshire lamb. If you're looking for something a bit different you can choose from a selection of tortilla wraps, and a number of vegetarian options (including Stilton and vegetable

Drive and Stroll

crumble) are always available. The New Inn is open from 12 noon to 3 pm and from 5 pm to 11 pm (12 noon to 11 pm on Saturdays). Meals are served from 12 noon to 1.45 pm and from 5 pm onwards, though no food is available on Sunday evenings. Telephone: 01472 840270.

THE WALK

Stride straight past the barn and into the Wolds. Your track, firm but steep, climbs to a tiny copse, wheels to the right and continues on a new bearing. Do not follow the track when it bends left at a solitary tree but carry on straight ahead, now on a field edge footpath with a hawthorn hedge running to its left. This is a quite exhilarating stretch combining the feel of a real Wolds walk with a vast panorama of the whole coastal 'Marsh' below. Sharp eyes will pick out Grimsby's Dock Tower and Spurn Lighthouse on the far bank of the Humber. Having lost much of its height the path reaches a lane onto which you turn left, having first explored the deserted little church behind the yew and elderberry screen.

The lane leads into a private garden but your route is along a clear grassy path to the left of the drive. Back into open arable country once more this track climbs arrow-straight as far as a road. A few yards along the road turn left onto the signed bridleway and, keeping the hedge on your left, head towards **Stock Furlong**, the wood ahead of you.

Before the wood, however, a clear track shoots off to the right, this time with a hedge on its right. Simply follow this fine broad track across the plateau until it descends to a quiet lane, now in **Wold Newton**. Walk to the right, admiring the Victorian estate cottages, mainly brick-built, in this village hidden amongst the trees in the valley. To your left the tiny spire of the church peeps above the trees on the hillside. Reaching **Church Path Cottage** – a generous clue – pass discreetly through the garden and climb the pathway to the church gates. The yard is beautifully maintained, the stone walls of the church are bedecked with roses and ivy and Scots pines tower overhead.

Leave this sublime setting by a gate in the south-east corner of the yard and proceed along the high-level footpath above the gardens of the village. Maintain your direction when a firmer track joins from the right and, when you reach **South Farm**, head straight through the farmyard to rejoin the road below. Turning right onto the road pass the impressive **Grange,** with its large duckpond and look out for a gate on your left where a muddy track disappears into deep woods. This is the valley, steep sided and sheltered, shaded by deciduous woodland ranging from mighty beech to stripling birch. The going can be – shall we say – soft, but every step through this magical woodland is a joy, and one of the highlights of the **Wanderlust Way**, whose course you are now following.

 ⑤

Unless you have been lured by tracks leading left and right you eventually emerge into sunlight at the edge of open fields. Continue between the fields in the same direction, still in the valley, until you reach a double gate. The right of way now traces the edge of a series of gated pastures until **Beesby Wood** comes alongside, displaying many fine specimens of mature oak. At this point another bridleway shoots up the hill and round the back of the wood, offering a

possible alternative route. But better by far is to continue below the wood to the shrunken farming hamlet of **Beesby**. Here the acres to your right contain the earthworks of the former village.

 ⑥

Just past an old white stable on your left look carefully for a gate leading you into the wood. Zigzag steeply through the narrow belt of greenery and, emerging on the other side, continue straight ahead on the track to the right of a hedge. Reaching a T-junction turn right and rejoin your outward route. As you approach the barrel-roofed barn once more you are afforded one last chance to savour the sweeping views across the coastal lowlands to the ships entering and leaving the Humber in the distance.

Places of Interest Nearby

The heyday of the world's premier fishing port is recalled at the **National Fishing Heritage Centre** in Grimsby, brought to life by detailed character models. Telephone: 01472 323345.

An exhibition and observatory at the **Discovery Centre** in neighbouring Cleethorpes details the wildlife along this coast. Telephone: 01472 323232.

19 Great Limber and Brocklesby Park

The mausoleum at Brocklesby Park is built on an ancient burial tumulus.

The Walk 3½ miles
Terrain An easy route on grass and good woodland tracks.
Map OS Explorer 284 Grimsby, Cleethorpes and Immingham or Landranger 113 Grimsby (GR 133087)

How to get there

Great Limber is situated 12 miles west of Grimsby on the A18. **Parking:** The Brocklesby Estate Walk car park in Great Limber, on the opposite side of the main A18 from Church Lane.

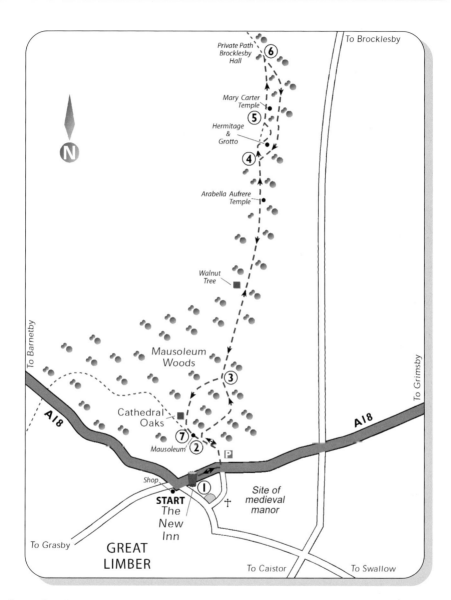

Introduction

Most Lincolnshire folk know of Brocklesby Hall, of its rich hunting heritage, and that it is not open to the public. What few will realise, though, is that Brocklesby Park is open from 1st April to 31st August. By entering the estate

Drive and Stroll

at its southernmost limit in Great Limber a privileged stroll through the wooded estate can be enjoyed. Although the Hall itself remains hidden, this magical walk begins and ends with a stunning piece of Wyatt architecture and is punctuated by fascinating curiosities. The woods were originally laid out to a design by Capability Brown and are nowadays so well managed they have been declared 'silviculturally outstanding' by the Forestry Commission. So, although you can only do this walk at a particular time of the year, I think you'll agree that it is well worth its place in this book.

The New Inn

This imposing Georgian hostelry enjoys pride of place at Great Limber's crossroads, across from the swaying trees of Brocklesby's private estate. Your meals can be eaten either in the long elegant restaurant or the more casual lounge, where ledges and shelves are stacked with books and other reading matter. Grimsby haddock, of course, is on the menu, though the steak and kidney suet pudding is also very popular, as are the steaks, chicken and duck – all served with delicious sauces. Lighter meals and snacks, Sunday lunches and Batemans' beers are all available – booking is recommended for Sunday lunch. The New Inn is open from 11 am to 3 pm and from 6 pm to 11 pm (open all day Friday to Sunday). Food is served from 12 noon to 2 pm and from 6.30 pm to 8.30 pm. Telephone: 01469 560257.

THE WALK

N.B. This walk is only open from 1st April to 31st August (see Introduction).

A tour of Great Limber village should be included in the day's itinerary. A weathered church set behind a willow-shaded pond, an old medieval manor site and a selection of estate cottages featuring candy twist chimneys and the Brocklesby crest are among the highlights of a village stroll.

From the car park, a narrow path shoots up into the woods behind the lawned clearing. Emerging from the greenery you are confronted by the most amazing spectacle. Crowning the hill in front of you is the **Brocklesby Mausoleum**, a domed masterpiece built of glowing stone and completely unexpected in the Lincolnshire landscape.

The mausoleum is itself built on an ancient burial tumulus and is regarded as Wyatt's masterpiece. Rarely seen is Nollekens' marble statue of Sophia Aufrere enshrined inside, a tragically romantic memorial to the wife of the first Lord Yarborough, who died in 1786 at the tender age of 33. If you are ever

The New Inn at Great Limber.

there on Brocklesby's annual open day do not miss this!

After admiring the mausoleum set off down the broad grassy slope between the trees of **Mausoleum Wood**. If uncertain, you are effectively performing a right-hand turn from the path by which you first entered this clearing. As you descend you will become aware of an enormous variety of trees surrounding you, though larch and pine mixed with broadleaves such as oak, beech and ash.

Where the route narrows and becomes firmer underfoot make a mental note of a route branching to the left, as this will form part of your return leg. A little further on look out on the left for a plaque by a walnut tree planted in 1938 to commemorate the 30 millionth tree since planting began in 1787. A few hundred paces beyond here a break in the woodland permits open views over the fields to the left, while on your right a small temple appears. This is the **Arabella Aufrere temple**, also accredited to Wyatt.

Past here look carefully on your right for a pathway leading to a decaying octagonal **hermitage** set in a glade by a large laurel tree. Peer inside to see the original rough-hewn tables and chairs. The path through the glade continues into the **Grotto**, a roughly carved and fearfully dark tunnel. On the other side of the Grotto the pathway reaches a track which you follow left to rejoin the main route through the woodland.

⑤

Turning right onto this, another temple is soon reached – dedicated to **Mary Carter** – and another chance to enjoy the views towards the Wolds. Just past here the walk ends with an arboreal flourish at a colossal sequoia and a 'Private' sign – the Hall itself tantalisingly close but remaining unseen.

⑥

About turn. Do not return along the same route, selecting instead a clear grassy swathe cutting through the woods to the left of the main track. Passing a selection of astonishingly tall trees, you arrive at the decaying trunk of a Wellingtonia Gigantia.

The tree is an eerie monument to the crew of a Lancaster Mark III shot down in flames by German aircraft on the night of 3rd March, 1945. The plane struck the tree and all seven crew members perished – a plaque here lists their names and ages, all between 19 and 33-years-old.

The next item to look out for is a series of marker posts on the right leading you, once again, back to the main track. Now simply retrace your steps all the way to the junction you noted earlier (point 3). Fork right here and continue until the woodland track opens out into a large grassy area, with a curious square plantation directly ahead of you.

The trees in the plantation, known as the Cathedral Oaks, were planted towards the end of the last century. When mature, they will provide timber for the future restoration of Lincoln Cathedral.

⑦

Ambitious walkers are informed that from this point it is possible to follow the serpentine belt of woodland for a number of miles, as far as **Brompton Dale Wood**. Otherwise your objective could not be more clear – the mausoleum appears once more atop its hill, framed by splendid cedars. This breathtaking sight is a fitting climax to the day's walk. Now climb the hill and return along the short wooded footpath to the car park.

Place of Interest Nearby

Six miles to the north is **Thornton Abbey**, where you are free to wander around the substantial ruins. The spectacular 14th-century gatehouse opens its doors to the public on certain summer days. Telephone: 01652 657053.

20 Susworth and Laughton Forest

The Beech Avenue at Tuetoes Hills in Laughton Forest

The Walk 2 miles (or 4 miles if you walk from the inn)
Terrain Fairly level walk on good forest tracks.
Map OS Explorer 280 Isle of Axholme or Landranger 112 Scunthorpe and Gainsborough (GR 836022)

How to get there

Scotter is 6 miles south of Scunthorpe on the A159. From here take the signed road on the right to Susworth. Tuetoes Hills Wood is 3 miles along here. A turning on the left, signed Laughton, leads into trees. **Parking:** Park in the first clearing on the left, opposite the site of the former car park. Otherwise, use the new car park, 400 yards south of here.

Drive and Stroll

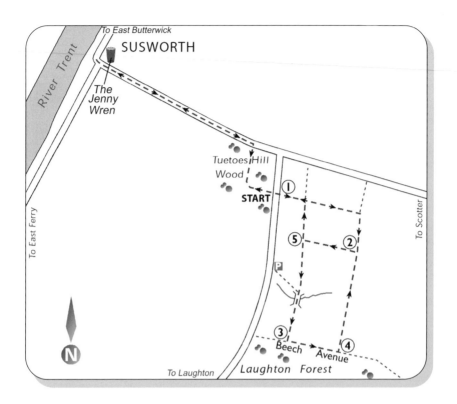

Introduction

Vast woodlands have replaced the sandy wind-blown heathland to the east of the River Trent. However, the sheltered paths that criss-cross the forest floor below make for a magical walk and a chance to spot rare flora and fauna along the way. By way of contrast, the open landscape of the mighty Trent's riverbank is close by the Jenny Wren, a delightful inn of historic origin and long-standing reputation. Before leaving the Jenny Wren, it is worth ascending the levee to survey the broad slow waters of the Trent – maybe you'll be lucky enough to see the Aegir, the Trent's tidal bore, as it rushes past.

The Jenny Wren

Since it was built in the 17th century, the Jenny Wren inn has enjoyed a chequered history. Originally a farmhouse, it later prospered as a ropery and store in the days when the Trent steam packet halted at Susworth on its way to Gainsborough. Today the inn consists of a series of immaculately laid out dining alcoves radiating from the central bar. The meals, too, are special – locally sourced where possible and freshly cooked. Steaks in mouth-watering sauces are a speciality, and the delicious Sunday roasts are so popular that booking ahead is advisable. The inn is open from 12 noon to 3 pm and from 6 pm to 11 pm (open all day on Saturdays and from 2 pm to 10.30 pm on Sundays). Meals are served from 12 noon to 2 pm and from 6 pm to 9 pm (12 noon to 9.30 pm on Saturdays and 12 noon to 8 pm on Sundays). The inn does not open on Mondays, except Bank Holidays. Telephone: 01724 784000.

THE WALK

Enter the wood via the narrow path leading east. The way becomes wider beyond the first crossing where the acres to the right are currently undergoing a clearance and replanting programme. When this track terminates, turn right and continue until the greenery on your left gives way to an arable field.

A few yards along the fence a clear path leads off to the right. Follow this path until it also terminates at a broader sandy track, onto which you turn left. When the sandy surface becomes stony do not deviate from your bearing but continue onto the rougher track ahead. A stream is crossed and the mighty pines give way to young deciduous trees – primarily birch. Proceed until, once again, your pathway ends – this time at a good stone track.

Turn left and stroll along this avenue lined with mature beech trees and a bank and ditch to either side – an unexpected change in surroundings and particularly dramatic in low winter sunlight. The woods of **Laughton Forest** on your right are private property.

Laughton Forest is a huge area of woodland planted on what was originally open heathland. The forest was acquired by the Forestry Commission in 1927 and planted with mainly coniferous trees. The whole region is abundant in wildlife, though only the Tuetoes Hills section is open to the public. Elusive woodpeckers and nightjars, interesting fungi and roe deer may be spotted. Nearby Hardwick Hill is the woodlands' highest point – a metal-working factory from the time of the Roman occupation has been unearthed here.

Reaching the second red post on the right, seek an obvious path leading off to the left. Beyond an area of Scots pines the path enters a plantation of young pine trees whose needles carpet the way and fill the air with their fresh scent. The path soon joins the fence bordering the open field once more and, when you arrive at the point at which you turned off earlier, repeat the

Drive and Stroll

The Jenny Wren Inn at Susworth has an interesting history.

exercise and follow the pathway away from the field as far as the T-junction.

This time turn right onto the sandy track and follow it back to the crossing encountered on the outward journey. Now turn left and retrace your steps along the narrow path through the undergrowth. Emerging from the foliage you have now arrived back at the roadside parking spot.

Now choose – drive or stroll to the Jenny Wren for refreshments? Walkers can cut the corner by continuing on along a track through the trees, swinging into a cleared area to reach the lane by a bar gate. Turn left to walk down the road to the Jenny Wren, returning by the same route.

Places of Interest Nearby

In **Scunthorpe** you will find an award-winning museum tracing the area's fascinating history. Telephone: 01724 402871.

Mount Pleasant Windmill at Kirton Lindsey, 8 miles to the east, was restored in 1991 and produces a full range of stone-ground flours. Telephone: 01652 640177.